H THE OLLOW ARMY

Recent Titles in
Contributions in Military Studies

U.S. Unilateral Arms Control Initiatives: When Do They Work?
William Rose

Transfer of Arms, Leverage, and Peace in the Middle East
Nitza Nachmias

Missile Defenses and Western European Security: NATO Strategy, Arms Control, and
Deterrence
Robert M. Soofer

The U.S. War Crimes Trial Program in Germany, 1946–1955
Frank M. Buscher

Democracy under Siege: New Military Power in Latin America
Augusto Varas, editor

Not Shooting and Not Crying: Psychological Inquiry into Moral Disobedience
Ruth Linn

"Seeing the Elephant": Raw Recruits at the Battle of Shiloh
Joseph Allan Frank and George A. Reaves

Civilian Indoctrination and the Military: World War I and Future Implications for the
Military-Industrial Complex
Penn Borden

Arms Race Theory: Strategy and Structure of Behavior
Craig Etcheson

Strategic Impasse: Offense, Defense, and Deterrence Theory and Practice
Stephen J. Cimbala

Feeding the Bear: American Aid to the Soviet Union, 1941–1945
Hubert P. van Tuyll

Military Planning for the Defense of the United Kingdom, 1814–1870
Michael Stephen Partridge

H THE OLLOW ARMY

*How the U.S. Army
Is Oversold and Undermanned*

WILLIAM DARRYL HENDERSON

Foreword by Charles Moskos

Contributions in Military Studies, Number 93

GREENWOOD PRESS

New York • Westport, Connecticut • London

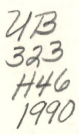

Library of Congress Cataloging-in-Publication Data

Henderson, William Darryl.
The hollow army : how the U.S. army is oversold and undermanned /
William Darryl Henderson ; foreword by Charles Moskos.
p.   cm. — (Contributions in military studies, ISSN 0883-6884 ;
no. 93)
Includes bibliographical references.
ISBN 0-313-26874-6 (lib. bdg. : alk. paper)
1. United States. Army—Personnel management. 2. United States.
Army—Combat sustainability. 3. Military education—United States.
4. United States. Army—Unit cohesion. I. Title. II. Series.
UB323.H46   1990
355.6'1'0973—dc20   89-23286

British Library Cataloguing in Publication Data is available.

Library of Congress Catalog Card Number: 89-23286
ISBN: 0-313-26874-6
ISSN: 0883-6884

First published in 1990

Greenwood Press, Inc.
88 Post Road West, Westport, Connecticut 06881

Printed in the United States of America

♾™

The paper used in this book complies with the
Permanent Paper Standard issued by the National
Information Standards Organization (Z39.48–1984).

10 9 8 7 6 5 4 3 2 1

Copyright Acknowledgment

Figure 8.1 in this volume is reprinted courtesy of *Army Times,* Copyrighted by Times
Journal Publishing Company, Springfield, Virginia, Aug. 8, 1988 edition, p. 4.

For Mary Ann

CONTENTS

FIGURES AND TABLES

FIGURES

TABLES

FOREWORD

A conventional wisdom defines the state of the U.S. Army today. It goes something like this. The Army was in bad shape coming out of the Vietnam War. Troop indiscipline, race strife, widespread drug abuse, among other maladies, all undercut soldier effectiveness. The end of the war and the draft in 1973 did not change matters very much. The early years of the all-volunteer force saw the education levels and test scores of recruits plummet, widespread recruitment scandals, and record levels of bad discharges and desertions in peacetime. But a major turnaround began in the early 1980s. High quality young people were again entering the Army; training was effective; soldiers were enthused; morale soared. Indeed, by the late 1980s, the U.S. Army was "the best ever." So goes the official story.

Colonel W. Darryl Henderson challenges that story. *The Hollow Army: How the U.S. Army Is Oversold and Undermanned* presents a compelling case of military malorganization. The evidence given here differs from the Pollyannaish glow of the public accounts on the recovery of the Army in the 1980s. *The Hollow Army,* however, is not muck raking. Nor is it an indictment of individual malfeasance or laxity. What we have here is an unusually well documented argument for the proposition that the Army's deep troubles in the way it prepares its soldiers for war are systemic.

The Hollow Army is all the more deserving of our attention because it alerts the reader not to noisy and well-publicized problems of the Army, such as in the latter years of the Vietnam War and the early years of the all-volunteer force. Rather, Colonel Henderson points to a quiet, and therefore more insidious, sort of crisis. *The Hollow Army* presents data, most of which has never before appeared in a public medium, revealing a series of interrelated problems: no constituency for manpower, personnel and training in the Army's budget fights; an inability to mass adequate "trigger pulling" combat soldiers; training that does not build on past lessons; high personnel turnover in all units; low cohesion in combat units; a concentration of less than competent sergeants in combat units; a promotion system that drives good sergeants out of the Army; and a low evaluation of the combat role despite lip service to the contrary.

The power of this book lies in Colonel Henderson's unique, indeed unrivaled, qualifications. If the sobriquet soldier-scholar fits anyone, it fits the author of *The Hollow Army*. As a young captain, Henderson commanded a rifle company in Vietnam during 1966–67. He suffered a near mortal personal attack by North Koreans on the Demilitarized Zone in 1975. But Colonel Henderson brings more than direct combat experience to this book. He holds a Ph.D. in comparative and international politics. He is the author of *Why the Viet Cong Fought* (1979), a provocative and convincing study of one of the most effective armies of modern times, and *Cohesion: The Human Element in Combat* (1985), a comparative analysis of four quite different armies, those of the United States, Israel, North Vietnam, and the Soviet Union.

Colonel Henderson's last Army assignment prior to retirement was Commander of the U.S. Army Research Institute for the Behavioral and Social Sciences. In that command, Colonel Henderson oversaw and monitored a wealth of social science data pertaining to Army manpower and training processes. As in his previous books, Colonel Henderson's *The Hollow Army* blends the critical insights of the professional soldier with factual documentation of the social scientist.

At the outset, it must be noted that *The Hollow Army* sets itself apart from the prevailing viewpoints on combat motivation and the dominant tendencies in military manpower policy. By making combat effectiveness the focus, Colonel Henderson gives little support to those who see advancing military technology revolutionizing warfare to the extent that the social psychological process of small groups of men in tactical situations are secondary considerations. Unlike too many others, Colonel Henderson regards the impending disappearance of the ground combat soldier in modern warfare to be greatly exaggerated.

The Hollow Army must also be placed in the context of theoretical studies of military sociology. Broadly speaking, studies of armed forces and society usually proceed along one or the other of two levels of analyses. On the one hand, the analysis focuses on the societal, cultural, and political context of military systems; on the other, the emphasis is on the internal organization of the military system. Whether or not one views the armed forces as an independent or dependent variable shapes policy conclusions as well. What distinguishes Colonel Henderson's study is that it gives due attention to both factors. The military is not treated in isolation from the societal context; at the same time, the unique qualities of the military organization are clearly kept in mind. Colonel Henderson bridges the gap between the level of micro-analysis based on individual behavior and the level of macro-analysis based on variables common to sociology.

I wish I could say that I am sure that the lessons of this book will be absorbed by the world of military consultants and those responsible for manpower policy at the highest levels. Yet, I fear that the reception that *The Hollow Army* will be accorded will show that the Army will not face up to the basic internal contradiction to which Colonel Henderson points. Namely, that the Army's overriding combat function is juxtaposed with a manpower and training system that systematically deemphasizes, if not degrades, combat soldiers and small-unit combat leaders. Colonel Henderson goes against the grain. He brings clarity to Army organizational features that are literally life-and-death matters.

PREFACE

The Vietnam experience was a unique chapter in U.S. Army history. It was the first war the Army did not "win." In fact, the Army emerged from the Vietnam era institutionally on its knees. In significant part, this was caused by expedient and shortsighted internal policies that weakened and allowed to unravel the human fabric that bound the Army together. The Army has since passed through two institutional phases of development. The first was the late 1970s' era of the "hollow Army" with its grave problems of poor discipline and performance and unusually high numbers of low-quality personnel measured in terms of mental capability. The next, beginning in the early 1980s, was the self-proclaimed Army of excellence, dramatized by higher-quality personnel with a marked improvement in discipline and performance.

While its architects and proponents are still actively building and promoting the new quality Army, it appears to some that this phase also has run its course. Essential to maintaining this second phase has been the marketing or selling of the new quality Army to the U.S. public, the Congress, and internally, to the Army itself. The marketing orders have been to tell the Army's story, and the fine print has been to be upbeat and positive, to tell only the story of the glass half-full. This marketing effort has been enormously successful. As a result, it is currently accepted by most who follow defense issues that the U.S. Army has never been better. The Army has even been pronounced, without question or objection, the best Army in the world, while in fact it has not risen above average to mediocre levels of performance.

It is the endeavor of this book to set in motion the next phase of the Army's evolution, which is needed if the Army is to achieve standards of performance necessary to win. This book describes the U.S. Army that exists at the beginning of the decade and one that will exist well into the 1990s before projected cuts cause significant changes. Unfortunately current indications are that the Army plans to make "balanced" cuts, essentially maintaining current malorganization and policies. A thesis of this book is that this course would be a major mistake. The current Army is not the best Army ever, and this will become apparent as the following chapters present the real Army story of the glass more than half empty and in need of significant change.

It is difficult to challenge the institution I have served for twenty-six years and the people I respect. But a long-standing commitment to Army and country demands that these critical issues be aired for public attention and discussion. The evidence is there. It requires that we hear and weigh it. Most important of all, it requires that we have the will to act.

I would like to acknowledge the help of, but leave unnamed for obvious reasons, the many superb researchers and analysts on manpower, personnel, and training issues found in organizations throughout the Army. Likewise, my thanks to my fellow soldiers; officers, sergeants, and troopers who have greatly influenced me over the years. A special note of thanks must go to Charles Moskos, a longtime mentor, for his generous help and comments on the manuscript. Additionally, the caveat that I alone am responsible for what is presented here is appropriate. However, it must be noted that many of the numbers presented reflect only a snapshot of constantly changing situations and should not detract from the more important and broad trends, findings, and interpretations presented.

Finally, this book could not have been written without the support of my family: my mother and father; my sons, Greg and Tim, who always made a point of following my progress and giving encouragement; and especially my wife, Mary Ann, who is at once my best critic, supporter, and editor.

THE HOLLOW ARMY

1

INTRODUCTION: SELLING A MYTHICAL ARMY

Every day some part of the U.S. Army's leadership "goes to market." They are "selling" a mythical Army to the Congress, the media, the American public, and to the Army itself. The message is that today's quality Army is the best Army ever — even that today's Army is the best in the world.[1] This theme is promoted by an enduring and widespread public affairs campaign intended to market the volunteer Army as a success. The specific content of the message is that the "Hollow Army" of the late 1970s with its low-quality personnel and related discipline and performance problems no longer exists. Instead, today, even with a slight drop in recruit quality in 1989, about 90 percent of the Army's incoming recruits are high school graduates, with over 60 percent above average (the highest percentage ever) in mental quality. Combined with a claimed 45 percent increase in combat power from a new generation of weapons systems such as the M-1 tank and the M-2 infantry fighting vehicle, the overall impression imparted is that indeed the Army is better than ever.

Not so! The U.S. Army is in the process of creating a myth lacking in substance. Just beneath the gloss of today's quality Army there exists a fault line with a potential fracture that could very quickly return the Army to the darkest days (1968–1980) of its recent history. This fracture, existing beneath the organizational surface, has its origin in long-buried and avoided MPT (manpower, personnel, and training) issues. In this context, manpower refers to numbers of soldiers. Personnel refers to soldier characteristics and organizational and policy decisions affecting their assignments and performance. Training refers to standards of combat unit performance.

At a time when the United States has just ended the biggest peacetime buildup of military power in its history, we are told that in the next war "we will fight outnumbered and with little, if any, technological superiority."[2] This squarely places the burden on the human element of the U.S. Army, and, as the Army enters the 1990s anticipating severe reductions, the substance of the various MPT issues developed in succeeding chapters is far from reassuring. Among the many MPT issues raised are the following:

- The "quality" soldiers of today's Army are, for the most part, only average or below average, when compared to the overall quality available in the American population and to the combat troops of other armies. In any event, their numbers are strategically insignificant.
- The Army can mass only about 85,000 combat troops from both active Army and reserve units capable of effectively fighting the first several months of any war.
- Combat unit performance as measured at the National Training Center remains average to mediocre.
- MPT policies ensure that combat unit training is short term, "event driven," and noncumulative.
- Personnel turbulence remains at the highest levels.
- The COHORT (Cohesion, Operational Readiness, and Training) program, designed originally to create strongly cohesive and high-performing units, was unable to overcome the vested policies of a deeply entrenched personnel bureaucracy and today must be considered a failure.
- Attrition remains very high and retention rates for top-quality first-term soldiers cannot meet future leadership requirements.
- In large part because of the Enlisted Personnel Management System (EPMS) and the Noncommissioned Officer (NCO) promotion system, combat units are not being adequately manned with high-quality noncommissioned officers.
- The sharp growth in officer and NCO ranks since the early 1970s has gone largely toward manning headquarters elements and centralized agencies at the expense of units.
- Basic assumptions rooted in managerial theories of the 1960s and 1970s continue to guide Army thinking about organization, and have resulted in a massive and sluggish centralized MPT bureaucracy, with no outside MPT constituency, which prevents attempts at reform such as the COHORT program from succeeding.

The situation outlined is in sharp contrast with the newly created mythical U.S. Army. Through adopting the commercial tactic of marketing, the Army has created a dangerous myth. Today's new quality Army, often presented as being the best Army ever, is a result of top leadership adopting marketing techniques to sell their programs. Top leaders believe "marketing sells the Congress,"[3] and have accepted marketing techniques to advance their programs with a number of target audiences to include the Congress, the media, the public, and perhaps most significantly, the rest of the Army. Top-level staffs attend seminars on how to market programs and messages. Staff officers are being sent to marketing courses. Failures of Army programs are being described as marketing failures. High-level leaders are forming "small groups to work on . . . imaging" in order to "sell" the vision of the new Army.[4] Repeatedly, officers and high-ranking civilians are urged to focus on and present the Army story as the glass that is half-filled with water, not half empty. This strategy has been effective because the criteria (e.g., quality soldiers) by which success is judged are marketed at the same time. Therefore, the volunteer Army is evaluated according to self-selected criteria. By these measures it is a success. But what is ignored is "The Dark Side of War" as described in the *Washington Post* recently,[5] and more importantly, the criteria needed to win in such wars. Almost every media story and much commentary on Capitol Hill begins with an acknowledgment that we now have the best Army ever, or at least a greatly improved Army that would be difficult to improve upon. The high percentage of quality soldiers now being recruited, the fact that over 90 percent of today's recruits are high school graduates, and the impressive performance of the Army's new weapons systems are most frequently cited as evidence in support of the myth that the Army has never been better.

However, the real issue is whether the whole story is being told or just the story of the glass half-full. Many midlevel officers tend to be wary of the "buyer beware" implications in the half-a-story marketing approach. There are sincere reservations about employing sales techniques developed for marketing commercial products to the public over the traditional military staff approach of presenting all the facts and then making the decision. However, the sad fact is that in an organizational environment where basic functions have been excessively fragmented among competing staffs and few have the power to make decisions, most issues have to be endlessly staffed, "sold," and finally compromised.

In such an organization, the good news is heavily marketed, the bad news is buried — not necessarily through deception but through lack of attention — it doesn't sell well. Researchers have received phone calls from general officers stating that they were going to brief the Chief of Staff or another high-ranking leader, and they wanted to know if there was any good news they could pass on in a particular area. The appetite among Army leaders for good news is well known. It is passed rapidly along up the chain of command. In fact, good news is carefully managed. Those who possess good news carefully pick their target audience for marketing effect and often personal credit. Good news tends to gather many sponsors and it is related to many programs. Good news spreads rapidly, often taking only hours to circulate throughout the Army while bad news tends to languish, taking weeks and months to move through a single staff section in a process seemingly reserved for bad news. First, it moves very slowly because it is checked and rechecked for accuracy and validity as a reason for dismissal. If it persists, then it tends to be compartmentalized and considered an isolated issue. Certainly there is little attempt to view such news from a systems perspective, and relate it and its effects to the overall system. As time passes, bad news that has been isolated, compartmentalized, and rationalized tends to sit there receiving little attention from the staff until it is displaced by the pace of events, and it gradually becomes buried and forgotten in the day-to-day process of the Army staff. General officers tend to become "front men" for their staffs in this process. With a 50 percent turnover rate among general officer positions each year and demanding schedules, the Army's leaders tend to become swept along with the inertia of the ongoing system and its mythology with little time or incentive to examine bad news in depth and relate it to an overview of the Army mission and status.

There is little to challenge the inertia of the present system. MPT issues receive little in-depth attention outside of the Army and the Defense Department. The broad components of a defense establishment are: a national strategy, military forces or manpower to execute the strategy, and the provision of weapons and materials to arm and supply the forces. Manpower issues have no widespread and continuing constituencies that fully explore and develop MPT issues as do strategic and weapons development and acquisition issues. The issues of national strategy are fully discussed beyond the Defense Department. In fact, U.S. strategy for the most part has been developed outside of the Defense Department. It has captured the interest of academia, think tanks, the Congress, and the media. As a result, the Defense Department has been well assisted in formulating and adjusting the strategy of deterrence over the years. The same is true of weapons systems development and acquisition. The large amounts of money involved ensure that the R&D community, industry,

Congress, and the media closely track and fully explore the development and acquisition issues involved in arming and supplying the U.S. Army. Comparatively, MPT issues receive little attention and this should not be considered unusual. Without the intrinsic interest of strategy or the dollars involved in weapons acquisition, MPT issues have little to attract outside interest. Moreover, manpower and personnel issues are usually expensive and often involve painful decisions that offer many liabilities and few advantages for any potential constituency. As a result, these issues attract comparatively little outside interest, and are usually left to a large and powerful, but sluggish, internal personnel bureaucracy that has developed tremendous inertia and markets a vested interest in the status quo very well. As a result, the manpower and personnel area has become the weakest part of the Army organization with many buried bad news issues that would quickly surface in a crisis and severely limit Army warfighting capabilities.

What follows in succeeding chapters is the accumulated bad news in the area of Army manpower, personnel, and training. All of the information presented here has been presented to the Army leadership over the past few years. It has generally passed the accuracy, reliability, and validity tests, yet it has been compartmentalized, isolated, and buried or forgotten. The following chapters take this basic information and follow it back into the organization of the Army, relating it to issues such as soldier quality, unit performance, and Army personnel policies. In turn, the implication of these MPT issues on U.S. strategy and the further implications for these issues on the Army's mission and warfighting capability are examined.

Chapter 2 begins the bad news with the thesis that the nature and significance of the Army's mission are changing and becoming much more important within recently evolving U.S. defense strategy. The protection provided by the nuclear umbrella, especially the intermediate nuclear force (INF) in Europe, was formidable and credible. They shielded many conventional force shortcomings, especially a wide range of Army MPT faults. However, with arms control and reduced tensions with the Soviet Union, the strategic balance and especially our Third World interests are becoming more dependent on conventional forces. The mismatch between evolving strategic requirements and present conventional capabilities is becoming apparent. There is a need to recast U.S. strategy and recognize the central role that has to be played by conventional forces and the Army. Any such shift in strategy should also recognize and accommodate the significant shortcomings in present U.S. conventional forces, especially those in the MPT areas.

Chapter 3 explores the actual numbers of combat troops or "trigger pullers" reasonably expected to be available from both the reserve and active army under a "competing strategies"[6] approach and concludes that the U.S. Army is no longer able effectively to employ the most important Principle of War, the Principle of Mass. With a Total Army organization of almost 2 million people, but inefficiently organized in a trigger puller to non-trigger puller ratio of one to twenty-three, the Army's resulting ability to mass only a total of approximately 85,000 trigger pullers from both reserve and active forces severely limits U.S. strategic options. From this number it is estimated that the greatest number of trigger pullers the Army could gather for the first several months of war is about 70,000. In all probability, Army planners would be very reluctant to commit the 82nd Airborne Division and other elements that comprise the Army's strategic reserve early in any conflict. This is probably true also for the 2nd Infantry Division in Korea, the 25th Infantry Division in Hawaii, and the 193rd Infantry Brigade in Panama. In any event, these forces would contribute very few trigger pullers to the Army's capability to mass. These numbers should not be surprising given recent trends in Army force structure. For example, there are now more Army signalmen assigned in Europe than there are infantrymen, and the Signal and Administrative branches have become far larger than the total numbers of artillerymen and tankers in the Army.

The overall effect is a serious shortcoming in a region of the world where the history of who wins and who loses wars has historically been determined by armies numbering in the hundreds of thousands and millions. The assumption is given that the Soviets, or for that matter any well-armed Third World adversary, with its own version of competing strategies (i.e., matching their strength against American weaknesses), could rely on their doctrine of surprise, mass, and speed to initiate, win, and conclude a war before the United States could even begin to sort out its MPT problems.

As a result, the present U.S. Army cannot reasonably expect to be effective in war except for lower spectrum of conflict type war. It appears to be limited to such wars as tidying up around the Caribbean, as in Grenada where it was able to get in and out quickly against a minimal force.

The Army response being marketed as the solution to its MPT problems centers on recruiting quality soldiers, high-tech weapons, and relying more on the reserve components under a "Total Army" concept. In fact, the great majority of today's "quality" soldiers come from the middle and bottom thirds of the U.S. population in terms of mental capability and performance. This does not match the quality available to other armies. Additionally, the improved soldier quality that has been achieved has not resulted in sustained higher levels of unit performance. Chapter 3 concludes that the reserve components as presently comprised, resourced, and trained cannot meet the role given them within the Total Army. Finally Chapter 3 suggests that manpower and dollar limits, which everyone recognizes and understands, are made much more burdensome by the recent and rapid growth of a burgeoning centralized Army bureaucracy characterized by increasingly fragmented and duplicative functions, especially in the personnel and supporting information management functions, consuming tens of thousands of personnel positions and hundreds of millions of dollars, with little or no increase in Army warfighting capacity.

Chapter 4 presents considerable evidence that in spite of a very sophisticated training establishment, the U.S. Army has erected organizational barriers that constrain the training establishment and keep most U.S. units on a training treadmill, unable to rise above average to mediocre levels of performance. As a result, training in the U.S. Army remains focused at the individual soldier level while unit training is "event driven" and noncumulative, resulting in nascent short-term effects within the unit. Such a training system calls into question the value received for the billions of dollars, either already spent or programmed, in support of Army combat training centers such as the National Training Center (NTC). The chapter concludes that until many MPT issues, such as an ineffective COHORT program, personnel turbulence, small-unit leadership, and related Enlisted Personnel Management System problems are resolved, major system barriers will continue to preclude the achievement of sustained and superior unit performance.

Chapter 5 continues the basic thesis that, in spite of stated good intentions through COHORT and other programs, personnel turbulence remains uncontrolled, unmeasured, unreported, and seemingly unacknowledged. In the face of a personnel system bureaucracy with considerable vested interests in the current system, the Army has been unable effectively to come to grips with this tremendously debilitating and persistent characteristic of its personnel system. Significant effects of personnel turbulence can be found throughout the Army. For example, as seen later, the Soviets are much more efficient at achieving greater training benefits from lesser amounts of training, while the U.S. Army in preparing for international competitive events such as the Canadian Cup Trophy (a tank crew competition) must in effect remove its competing crews from the normal ongoing personnel and training systems in order to achieve the unit stability, leadership, and cumulative training necessary to be competitive in these events.

Chapter 6 reminds us that in order to win modern conventional war, with its immense firepower concentrated in small units, more than ever before dispersed, independent, small-unit actions must be led by small-unit leaders of the highest quality. The bad news is that for organizational reasons, today's small combat unit leaders are not providing the quality leadership necessary even to come close to maximizing the fighting potential of the Army's new weapons systems and the soldiers who man them.

The requisites necessary to achieve high standards of unit performance are closely linked to the small unit's capability to meet the soldier's social and support needs. Chapter 7 maintains that the current Army structure and personnel system make it very difficult to structure the cohesive units necessary to meet the soldier's needs, especially in a combat or extended conflict environment. The chapter concludes that the COHORT program, instituted several years ago with high expectations of improving unit cohesion, is today a failure. The changes necessary to fulfill the expectations for it were not possible in the face of a powerful personnel bureaucracy with enormous inertia and a considerable vested interest in the status quo. Most worrisome are the considerable data that indicate a potentially serious personal and professional break between small combat unit leaders and their soldiers. The data indicate that unit leaders have not been able to reach out to the individual soldier and bond him to the unit. Today's recruit who joins primarily for economic reasons or reasons related to personal gain is thrust into a unit that is incapable of providing the long-term leadership necessary to bind the soldier to the unit and the Army. Instead the soldier experiences an ever-growing lack of personal and professional respect for his immediate leaders and the professional Army values necessary for small units to win.

The results of the Army's self-initiated but failed attempts at internal reform such as COHORT and related EPMS programs have become most apparent within the NCO Corps. Chapter 8 reflects on the NCO Corps and how its primary function has changed over the past fifteen years to demonstrate the cumulative effects of an ever-growing centralized Army bureaucracy that is consuming enormous personnel and dollar resources with little increase in Army warfighting capability. For the NCO Corps, this has meant that their traditional functions of training and leading soldiers in war have been expanded to include the additional function of "junior staff officer." This additional function is required because of the fragmentation and duplication caused by a greatly expanded centralized

Army bureaucracy. Since 1973 the size of the midlevel (E–5–E–7) NCO Corps has increased mostly to man the additional headquarters, support agencies, information commands, and administrative staffs that have been added to support the centralization of functions within the Army. Unfortunately, in addition to paying the enormous manpower and dollar costs involved, the Army has given the highest priorities to these new NCO staff functions, assigning most of the top-quality NCOs to noncombat units. As a result the NCO Corps no longer primarily serves well its traditional function: the training and leading of small units in war. The tremendous warfighting potential of the NCO Corps is being lost through assignment to jobs that contribute little to warfighting; this leaves the U.S. Army unable to match the quality of small-unit leadership of other armies much smaller in size.

The final chapter concludes that present organizational limitations to Army warfighting capabilities contribute to the Army's inability to perform its stated mission and must be addressed if the Army is to achieve maximum value for the manpower and dollars allocated. It is suggested that a rigorous structural-functional systems analysis will identify surprisingly large amounts of manpower (in the tens of thousands) and dollars (in the hundreds of millions) that are contributing little to Army warfighting capability. A searching review is needed of the underlying assumptions that have led the Army to fragment, duplicate, and centralize many functions over the past years with little value added. The probability exists that the Army can take significant steps toward meeting its mission within the already programmed force structure budget.

NOTES

1. This theme is widely evident in almost all Army public affairs efforts over the past several years. Prepared scripts and guidelines are widely distributed, and the theme is almost always included in top leadership addresses to target audiences. For example, Delbert L. Spurlock, Jr., Assistant Secretary of the Army for Manpower and Reserve Affairs in "On the Record," *Army Times*, October 17, 1988, 22.

2. Briefing to Army officers by Lt. General Bartlett, Commander, Combined Arms Center, Ft. Leavenworth, Kans., September 14, 1987.

3. Deputy Chief of Staff for Personnel, U.S. Army, at staff marketing workshop, Ft. Meyer, Va., June 5, 1987.

4. Spurlock, memo for Chief of Staff (Subject: Army image), July 14, 1988, 4.

5. Fred Downs, "Death and the Dark Side of Command," *Washington Post*, Outlook section, August 16, 1988; and John F. Ahearne, "The Dark Side of War," *Washington Post*, August 23, 1987, p. B6.

6. The notion of "competing strategies" was introduced into discussions of defense issues by the Secretary of Defense in 1987 in his report to Congress for the 1988–1989 budget and appears to have been also adopted by the Bush administration as a continuing guide for defense strategy into the 1990s. Originated by Graham Allison, the basic concept was that enduring long-term American strengths in defense should be aligned to take full advantage of Soviet weaknesses. As implemented, the concept has largely been oriented toward directing U.S. technology and related weapons systems against Soviet weaknesses with little, if any, thought given to U.S. vulnerabilities (e.g., MPT issues) or how potential enemies, including those in the Third World, could implement a competing strategies approach of their own directed toward enduring U.S. vulnerabilities.

2

THE ARMY MISSION: A MISMATCH FOR TODAY'S ARMY

The mission of the U.S. Army, as often presented in Pentagon briefings, is shown as comprising three separate requirements in support of national strategy: (1) to deter attack along the entire spectrum of possible levels of conflict (see Figure 2.1), (2) to defeat any enemy if deterrence fails, and (3) to act globally in deterring or defeating any enemy.[1] Some variation of this mission is likely to remain even in view of the apparent erosion of the Iron Curtain and fundamental shifts in the balance of power between NATO and the Warsaw Pact nations. What is likely to change for the U.S. Army is a major reassessment and reduction of the resources, men, weapons, and materiels needed to accomplish this mission in view of the fundamental shifts in world power, military and economic, as the United States begins the 1990s.

Especially inappropriate for the new environment the Army must face are the Army's manpower, personnel, and training (MPT) practices. They are rooted in U.S. preparations for World War II and persist even though many are enormously expensive and ineffective. Forthcoming changes in the immediate future should be approached by the Army as an opportunity for open reassessment and restructuring necessary for a more effective and affordable Army. Unfortunately early signs are that the Army intends to muddle through by incremental adjustments of current MPT organizations and practices. Subsequent chapters make clear that the U.S. Army continues, especially in the MPT areas, to rely on what has become the traditional American method of preparing for war, described as follows by General Jones, former Chairman of the Joint Chiefs of Staff. "History books glorify our military accomplishments [but] a closer

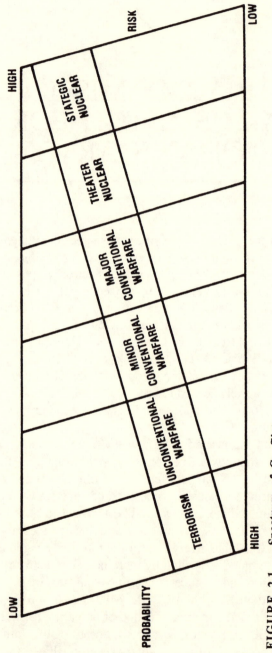

FIGURE 2.1 — Spectrum of Conflict

12

examination reveals a disconcerting pattern; unpreparedness at the start of the war; initial failures; reorganizing while fighting; cranking up our industrial base; and ultimately prevailing by wearing down the enemy, by being bigger not smarter."[2]

History is repeating itself in the Army's manpower, personnel, and training shortcomings outlined the following chapters. While weapons systems development and procurement progress relatively satisfactorily, in large part because of active business and congressional constituencies, Army MPT issues languish and are buried. Because MPT issues,especially manpower, involve large expenses, are often personally painful, and have no constituencies comparable to those supporting weapons procurement, there is a strong tendency to ignore these issues until, periodically, they can no longer be buried and they emerge in all of their alarming detail demanding reassessment.

Such a period of reassessment appears to be necessary now. The protection provided by the nuclear umbrella, especially the INF forces in Europe, was formidable and shielded many conventional force Army shortcomings, especially a whole range of MPT faults outlined in later chapters. With more arms control agreements likely, the focus is now on conventional force capabilities and their increased role in U.S. strategy. The broad outlines of the situation have been presented to Congress and described by National Security Advisor Brent Scowcroft as "fundamentally" changing the policy of deterrence, which has been the "bedrock of policy toward the Soviet Union for forty years."[3] Other well-known strategists and practitioners are also uneasy over recent and especially the future military situation it augurs. Former Secretary of State Henry Kissinger, former Supreme Allied Commander Europe (SACEUR) General Bernard Rogers, and House Armed Services Committee Chairman Les Aspin, have all expressed their unease.[4] They see a situation in which the shift away from reliance on nuclear weapons to a military situation requires "major improvements in conventional forces".[5] A basic assumption is that when the current era of change runs its course, conventional forces will be more important in maintaining the international balance of power over their subordinate position during the past forty years of nuclear deterrence. Although the future Army might be smaller its conventional role will have gained relative to that of nuclear forces and thus the importance of a first rate Army that achieves maximum combat power for the resources expended.

The assumptions underlying these positions are not unreasonable and would almost surely be reflected in the Soviet equivalent of our competing strategies approach. While the specific effects of the Soviet

50,000-troop reduction and other reductions in Eastern Europe announced by Gorbachev are not yet evident, it is clear that major changes are under way in the Soviet Union. Whatever course future Soviet-American relationships take, it seems certain the course will be characterized by great uncertainty on the international stage and unpredictability among its actors, accompanied by significant potential for increased risk and crises.

While it is becoming apparent that the Soviets believe the nuclear arena is largely stalemated and open for arms control agreements, there is no real evidence they believe conventional armed forces have lost their utility. Certainly the recent INF agreement has enhanced Soviet conventional capabilities. The potential impact of the changed conventional military situation has not gone unnoted in the West. Conventional arms control efforts notwithstanding, the importance of conventional forces will ascend in the 1990s as much conflict is perceived as being beyond the threshold of nuclear forces. Former Chairman of the Joint Chiefs Admiral William J. Crowe has characterized the imbalance in conventional forces as "horrifying."[6]

As the U.S.-Soviet relationship changes and develops and nuclear weapons become less useful in maintaining the peace, the Third World appears to be becoming more unruly and dangerous, with one out of four countries now engaged in some level of warfare.[7] At the same time conventional arsenals are growing, with over twelve countries in the Third World now maintaining armies with over 1,000 main battle tanks.[8] This should be especially worrisome to the United States because U.S. conventional forces are poorly structured and equipped for this type of conflict.[9]

In such an emerging international environment, the Soviet Union, or any Third World nation, attempting what the United States is attempting under its competing strategies approach — to align their enduring strengths against enduring American weaknesses — would almost assuredly take advantage of superior conventional forces in a manner that enhances strategic surprise. Soviet or other nations' ability to achieve surprise crucial to a strategy for short conclusive war emphasizing mass, speed, and surprise should not be doubted. Sufficient evidence is available to challenge those who maintain that national technical means (e.g., spy satellites) now preclude the possibility of achieving strategic conventional surprise.[10] Klaus Knorr and others point out that even if the most modern surveillance technology had been available, the Nazi occupation of Norway, the 1940 German invasion of the Soviet Union, the Vietnam Tet offensive, and the Egyptian attack into the Sinai in 1973, for example, would have occurred as they did. Problems with periods of reduced visibility (even using the latest satellites, launched in December 1989), improved methods of deception, lengthy processing and analysis delays, misinterpretation, and the imperative of the political over military logic (as in the Egyptian attack during Yom Kippur), as well as other factors, all contribute to the "fog of war" and can be of immense aid to strategies dependent upon surprise.

High technology is often seen as a major part of efforts to make conventional forces more capable, and in the context of current concerns about increased conventional vulnerabilities in the West, many in the United States are looking to technology for "silver bullets," to deter war or, if necessary, to help win wars. In the United States especially, strategy is becoming synonymous with high technology. A most recent example is the January 1988 bipartisan report by the Commission on Integrated Long-Term Strategy.[11] Of the several factors that comprise strategy, the commission looked almost exclusively to technology as the most promising means for the United States and the West to prevent or win conventional war. Developing pinpoint delivery of immensely powerful conventional munitions with "smart" missiles was offered as one example of how conventional military power could come to fill the deterrence role vacated by nuclear weapons.

Historically technological solutions are appealing. World War II was won in part through advanced technology. At the heart of such an approach to strategy is that technology can overcome or at least neutralize military problems linked to the human element of strategy, especially the tendency in democracies to make do with minimal manpower and associated programs. In this context, recent discussion by senior Army leaders to sacrifice manpower to pay for new technology is understandable. As early as February of 1988, the undersecretary of the Army proposed letting Army strengths drop to 521,000 soldiers in order to pay for new weapons systems including "robotic" systems.[12] Never mind that it is doubtful that we can ever produce a robot with the artificial intelligence to successfully compete with enemy soldiers at the controls of a tank. This latest offering at the altar of military high technology does not take into account the current strategic situation with its operational, manpower, and training deficiencies. Of the four broad areas of strategy — operations, logistics, technology, and manpower or the human element — the United States has usually been most vulnerable in the last, and today, much more than usual. The relative decrease in U.S. military power since World War II and the most recent increase in the importance of conventional forces in the world arena, especially the Third World, has made the United States more vulnerable. The technological solution offered by the Commission on Integrated Long-Term Strategy and others falls short, especially as it concerns the U.S. Army.

In a comprehensive competing strategies approach all enduring enemy strengths are aligned against enduring American weaknesses, and enduring American strengths against enemy weaknesses.[13] The strategic analyst is forced to compare MPT elements of strategy as well as technology. However, the current U.S. approach to competing strategies is almost exclusively oriented toward directing U.S. technology and related weapons systems against Soviet weaknesses. Any reading of the U.S. approach to competing strategies makes apparent the almost total lack of consideration of manpower and related concerns. The implicit assumption appears to be that technology will let the Untied States continue to avoid the painful manpower questions associated with today's strategic posture. This view was openly expressed by the director of the Defense Advanced Research Projects Agency (DARPA). He stated:

> It's my view that this society has decided that it will only use a certain fraction of its human effort in its own defense or in preparation for its own defense in peacetime. The imperative just isn't there, we are what we are. We don't have the resolve . . . so consequently we have no other alternative but to turn to high technology. That's it.[14]

Currently this approach has reached a dangerous extreme for three reasons. First, for reasons discussed previously and much more widely in the strategic literature, today's strategic equation has shifted toward greater reliance on conventional forces. Second, technology does not appear to have much to offer conventional forces, and the available technology appears to be fairly evenly balanced worldwide. Third, U.S. armed forces in particular are still geared to a force structure more appropriate for a strategy primarily linked to theater and world nuclear deterrence and thus more forgiving of MPT deficiencies than a strategy in which conventional forces are in the fore.

The evidence that the United States should not expect great technological advantages in war is plentiful. The final report of the 1987 Defense Science Board Summer Study summarized the situation. "There is an increasing risk that the U.S. is losing the technological advantage on which we base our strategy for military superiority, and there is a growing perception that the Department of Defense is getting progressively less for the research and development dollar."

Current Pentagon estimates credit the Soviets, and, more importantly, many of their Third World customers, with technology roughly equivalent to that of the United States with a decided advantage in the areas of battlefield lasers, radar jammers, antiballistic defenses, and high-energy particle beams. Recent testimony and commentary by representatives of the U.S. armor community indicate that Soviet Army main battle tanks outmatch the best tank (M-1) the United States has in its inventory. Even after making some allowance for the Army lobby's attempting to get the attention of Congress, the message was alarming. In the context of the overall balance of conventional forces, Aspin, the chairman of the Armed Services Committee, has referred to it as a "very, very serious problem."

While it might appear easy to demonstrate that the United States and NATO have a sharp technological edge over the Soviets, it has been observed by a former Assistant Secretary of Defense for Research and Engineering that such advantage is mainly in the laboratory and industry but not in the field where soldiers will fight.[15] Through industrial priorities and technology from the West, the Soviets and many Third World nations consistently close the technology gap in warfighting capabilities.

Soviet near-parity in warfighting technology and their superior conventional forces make for an increasingly vulnerable military balance, especially in a strategic situation where the weight attributed to conventional forces is steadily greater. This situation is not discernible in U.S. Army briefings today. In fact, Army "marketeers" present charts reflecting a 45 percent increase in combat power achieved by the Army over the past several years. Such projections are a distortion of the actual warfighting situation; they are based on "bench science" projections of improved technology such as rates of fire, and so on. They do not include the human element and related MPT issues. Not only are gross inadequacies of numbers not included, but significant personnel and training problems that appear to be intractable under present organization and policies are excluded. Projections such as a 45 percent increase in warfighting capability, because of greater capabilities of systems like the M-1 tank and the M-2 infantry fighting vehicle, are the result of linear logic at best and dangerous distortion for marketing purposes at worst. In other areas, such as the MANPRINT program, which attempts to ensure that weapons systems are designed with human capabilities in mind, the Army recognizes that the most important factor in the warfighting equation is the soldier. Yet, consistently, the Army achieves less than maximum system performance because, according to Martin Binkin, "of the difficulties in operating and maintaining technologically advanced weapons systems with currently available personnel."[16]

It is suggested that the U.S. Army has begun to display characteristics of an overcentralized, top-heavy, comfortable bureaucracy with tremendous inertia and with little ability to conduct the critical self-examination necessary to address its growing list of organizational deficiencies. These factors, as discussed in succeeding chapters, have an enormous impact on Army warfighting capabilities and therefore on U.S. ability to successfully execute military strategies requiring conventional capabilities.

NOTES

1. Vice Chief of Staff, U.S. Army briefing to participants at the annual Soldier Performance Research and Analysis Review II, May 28, 1987. Figure 2.1.

2. General David C. Jones, Chairman of the Joint Chiefs of Staff, cited in Edward Luttwak, *The Pentagon and the Art of War* (New York: Simon and Schuster, 1985), 266.

3. Brent Scowcroft, cited by Rudy Abramson, "Eliminating Ballistic Missiles Dangerous," *Los Angeles Times,* December 6, 1986, 6.

4. Jeffery Record, *Armed Forces Journal* (October 1987): 76.

5. General John R. Galvin, Supreme Commander Allied Forces, Europe, cited by Henry Vanloon, *Armed Forces Journal* (March 1988): 50.

6. Admiral William J. Crowe, Jr., Chairman of the Joint Chiefs of Staff, cited by David Wood, "Kremlin Stealthily Amasses Strike Force in Europe," *Newark Star-Ledger,* December 8, 1987, 44.

7. William Matthews, "U.S. Seen Poorly Equipped for Low-Intensity Wars," *Army Times,* December 8, 1986, 12.

8. John Herrly, "Midweight Force Needed Now More than Ever," *Army Times,* May 15, 1989, 23.

9. Matthews, "U.S. Seen Poorly Equipped," 12.

10. Klaus Knorr and Patrick Morgan, eds., *Strategic Military Surprise* (New Brunswick, N.J.: Transaction Publishers, 1982), 247–65.

11. Report of the Commission on Integrated Long-Term Strategy, "Discriminate Deterrence" (Washington, D.C.: GPO, January 1988).

12. George C. Wilson, "Army Faces Deep Personnel Cuts to Pay for Arms," *Washington Post,* February 11, 1988, 4.

13. Report of the Secretary of Defense to Congress on the Fiscal Year 1988–1989 Budget and Fiscal Year 1989–1992 Defense Programs (Washington, D.C.: Department of Defense, January 12, 1987), 65–66.

14. Cited in William Darryl Henderson, *Cohesion: The Human Element in Combat* (Washington, D.C.: National Defense University Press, 1985), 17.

15. William Perry, cited by Len Famiglietti, "NATO Leaves Technology in Laboratory," *Jane's Defense Weekly,* November 28, 1987, 1245.

16. Martin Binkin, *Military Technology and Defense Manpower* (Washington, D.C.: The Brookings Institution, 1986), 68.

3

ARMY MANPOWER: AN ISSUE WITH NO CONSTITUENCY

According to Clausewitz, "the first principle of strategy" is to ensure "that as many troops as possible should be brought into the engagement at the decisive point . . . the first rule, therefore, should be; put the largest possible army into the field."[1] The U.S. Army agrees with Clausewitz. *Field Manual 100-5,* the Army's premier operations manual on how to fight wars, states that mass, as a principle of war, requires the Army to "concentrate combat power at the decisive place and time."[2] The same manual also describes "the next battlefield" as being characterized by "massive troop concentrations" making penetration inevitable.[3]

There is considerable evidence that the U.S. Army is no longer able effectively to employ this most important Principle of War, the Principle of Mass:

- Present U.S. Army inability to mass adequate troops (i.e., infantry, armor, artillery) in either active or reserve forces is a serious violation of Clausewitz's first rule and the principles of war.
- A Total Army strength of 760,000 active duty soldiers, 789,000 reserve component soldiers, and 412, 000 Army civilians, for a total of almost 2 million people organized in a trigger puller to non-trigger puller ratio of about one to twenty-three presents serious questions about manpower available for warfighting under current Army organization.
- A competing strategies approach makes clear that the severe limitations on U.S. Army ability to mass adequate combat troops significantly limits U.S. strategic options. The U.S. Army cannot

19

reasonably expect to be successful in wartime missions except for lower spectrum of conflict type war (e.g., Grenada).

- U.S. Army response to its manpower problems emphasizes recruiting quality soldiers and greater reliance on the reserve components under the Total Army concept. However, today's quality soldiers are in fact mostly average or below average while the reserve components are "choking" on their increased responsibilities under the Total Army concept.

- Improved individual soldier quality has not been translated into sustained higher levels of unit performance and has not yet proven to be the answer to the Army's warfighting manpower problems in spite of extensive marketing efforts.

- The high-quality soldiers recently recruited look impressive when compared to the previous low-end quality of the 1970s but today's combat unit quality is mostly average and below average, drawn from the middle and lower thirds of the U.S. population.

- Performance data from top one-third quality soldiers are significant when comparing the competing strategies of armies where one army has significantly more top-quality soldiers, especially in combat units.

- Low numbers of combat soldiers available for massing, persistent "economic man" motivation, high attrition rates, relatively few top one-third quality soldiers, and an ineffective COHORT program are reflected in low soldier commitment to units, leaders, and professional values, and low overall warfighting potential. The combined significance of these manpower factors for warfighting in the context of competitive strategies is enormous.

- Just as the highly marketed quality Army has not been the answer, the reserve components also cannot, as presently resourced, provide the answer to the total Army's significant manpower problems.

- The reserve components provide few combat-ready units available for massing.

- Those relatively few reserve component combat troops that are available are not traditional reserves but actually poorly trained soldiers in "deep hibernation," dedicated to active Army unit missions.

- The United States has no system to ensure that the top one-third of its citizens are available for defense through a reserve system similar to those of the German, Israeli, and Soviet armies.

- Inadequate training, rapid decay of complex skills, the questionable reliability of the Individual Ready Reserve (IRR), and the lack of a rapid train-up system for emergencies forecast inadequate reserve component warfighting capability.

- Total Army manpower problems of both active and reserve forces severely limit U.S. strategic options when the effects of these problems are related to the manpower implications of competing strategies.
- The effects of the manpower problems outlined have been made significantly more burdensome through the centralization of manpower, personnel, and training (MPT) functions and attendant support organizations, headquarters, and information commands at Department of Army level. The creation of a huge centralized Army bureaucracy often with fragmented and duplicative functions has consumed tens of thousands of personnel positions with little or no increase in warfighting capacity.

Manpower limitations, combined with how the Army organizes and utilizes its existent manpower, preclude the capacity to mass sufficient combat troops to engage successfully in warfare beyond the low-intensity range of warfare. Today's Army cannot be reasonably expected to be successful in executing missions that call for it to do more than small jobs such as tidying up around the Caribbean, as in Grenada. For example, the extreme reluctance of the Defense Department in 1988 to support State Department options for military pressure in Panama stemmed in large part from the significant strain even such limited options have on available manpower. Certainly the level of effort required by such missions as taking the field and defeating a determined army in the jungles of Central America, or defending the U.S. front in Europe in a conventional war, are beyond the capabilities of today's Army given an informed and reasonably well-executed competing strategy (e.g., an enemy strategy based on a comparison of competing strategies emphasizing doctrines of speed, surprise, and mass).

The combat power of an army is defined in U.S. Army *Field Manual 100-5* as including indirect sources of power such as leadership, training, and logistics. The principal means for an Army to focus or use such power is through massing combat troops whose primary function is to fire at the enemy. Logistics, leadership, technology, training, and other factors that underpin combat power cannot influence warfighting except through combat troops. While the effects of supporting soldiers and civilians may be included in an assessment of combat power, such power can only be indirectly employed through those combat troops whose primary purpose is to fire at the opposing forces. Therefore, to measure the capability of an Army to mass combat power, one must first focus on the actual numbers of combat troops (i.e., troops with the primary function of firing at the enemy) available to an army in both its active and reserve forces, accompanied by a supporting assessment of the leadership, cohesion, training, soldier capacity, weapons, technology, materials, and other indirect supporting factors available to or inherent in these combat troops. This chapter is concerned primarily with the numbers and the capabilities of such trigger-pulling troops available to the U.S. Army and uses this term interchangeably with combat troops.

Clausewitz recognized the importance of the relationship between combat troops and the various indirect factors inherent within the "military virtues" outlined earlier.[4] He stated that the "distribution of elementary military strengths" takes place "among the three main arms" of an army, which he identified as the infantry, artillery, and cavalry (i.e., armor and aviation).[5] The Principle of War then that we recognize as Mass, for Clausewitz was the actual numbers of infantry, artillery, and armor troops available for decisive engagement in combat. These troops with their inherent virtues and support were, for Clausewitz, the primary factors in assessing an army's ability to fight wars.

The inability of the U.S. Army to meet this first principle of Clausewitz and to mass adequate numbers of combat troops is not recognized widely within the U.S. Army. Those few who are aware of the deficiency generally do not link this organizational problem with broader strategic considerations. Vague thoughts of mobilization of the reserves and/or a last-minute draft are usually cited. Generally there is no acknowledgment that the total combat force reasonably expected to be available during the first months of war severely limits U.S. options for conventional response to the very lowest levels of response on the spectrum of possible types of conventional conflict. Additionally, there is no recognition that the forces eventually produced through mobilization would be of the lowest proficiency in terms of individual and unit skills, cohesion, and effective leadership, primarily because the production of these virtues requires many months, time that would not be available to the U.S. Army. Additionally, the present training base is unable to produce the necessary trained soldiers in wartime. The centralized production in just a few sites of individually trained soldiers, not trained units, is geared to maintaining the present force structure through an individual replacement system that would become a major bottleneck in war, the current package replacement system notwithstanding. Little has changed in the Army's personnel system since the Commander of Forces Command, with over 200,000 soldiers, wrote the Deputy Chief of Staff for Personnel in 1983 that: "It is obvious that the kind of centralization and paragraph/line number manipulation by MILPERCEN [Personnel Command] managers ... is totally unworkable and will not accommodate the requirement for a decentralized system that is needed for both peacetime and wartime operations."[6]

Any comparison of U.S. Army warfighting capability with potential enemy armies under the competing strategies approach must recognize that many potential enemies possess armies that are organized in a manner that ensures that far greater numbers of combat troops are available for massing and are organized in units that, because of higher quality, higher unit proficiency, and probably higher cohesion, are better prepared for warfighting than is our total Army. Performance data cited elsewhere (Chapter 4) support this view. Additionally, although their comments are muted, many of our allies believe much U.S. Army unit performance is not up to standards.

The stark warfighting limitations that currently limit U.S. strategy and capabilities are demonstrated best by examining present U.S. Army capability to mass trigger-pulling troops. Presently in Europe the U.S. Army can mass only approximately 28,000. From all of its current (eighteen) active divisions, the U.S. Army is capable of massing only approximately 50,000 trigger pullers.

The definition of combat troops used here conforms to Clausewitz's requisite for massing combat power and refers to those soldiers (infantry artillery, armor) who have as their primary function the task of firing at the enemy. This refers to trigger pullers such as tank crews, infantrymen, artillery crewmen, and others. It does not include soldiers whose primary missions are complementary, such as staff coordination, command and control, maintenance, supply, communication, or administration. In the aggregate then the Army has comparatively few trigger-pulling soldiers, and when these are gone they are not easily replaced. For a basic example, the problem can be followed back to the unit at platoon level. A fully manned infantry squad equipped with the Bradley fighting vehicle with a crew of three can only produce six infantrymen, often without a squad leader, for traditional dismounted infantry operations. A few years ago this number was eleven. However, given current manning levels this number is now about four when the three-man crew stays on the vehicle.[7] At a higher level it might be reassuring to speak of a light division and gain confidence from the military power usually associated with the term "division." However, some of today's active U.S. Army light divisions can put only about 1,500 trigger pullers in the field to fire at the enemy. In terms of the requirement to mass in modern warfare, this is insignificant. The problem for armor units is the lack of sufficient crews with high-quality leadership to man even the moderate number of tanks available to the U.S. Army. Given the realistic projection of over 100,000 U.S. casualties during the first thirty days of conventional warfare in Europe and the very low initial number of combat troops available to be massed for combat operations, the U.S. capability to mass any type of credible combat force in Europe or elsewhere for sustained conventional operations is doubtful.

The implications for the U.S. strategic positions under a comprehensive analysis of competing strategies are significant. These limitations extend to other areas. With reduced threat in Europe in 1989 the Army risked units reserved to Europe for operations in Panama. A lesson evident in 1990 from U.S. involvement in Panama is that significant numbers are required even for such limited operations. Almost any level of sustained resistance could quickly bring the U.S. Army to the limits of its ability to mass and sustain combat troops.

Leaving aside the lengthy, detailed, and to date inconclusive discussion on the proper combat to combat support or tooth-to-tail ratio and related arguments about complex technology, weapons systems, and required support, the determination of an army's real warfighting capability is determined by the numbers of combat troops deployable in quality units. The combat to combat support ratio is not the issue here except to say that both combat support (CS) and combat service support (CSS) units contribute to warfighting and that given a high support to combat troop strength ratio, a higher end-strength is necessary to support any given number of combat troops.

The real issue is the very low number of combat troops available for massing and, in view of the relatively large end-strength of the total Army (almost 2 million), the related need to identify those organizations that consume manpower but do not contribute significantly to the combat or combat support warfighting capacity of the U.S. Army. As noted, the active Army is only capable of massing approximately 50,000 trigger-pulling troops in combat units (with mixed unit proficiency) and about 85,000 total if reserve component combat units are included.[8] Considering that the total Army strength is 760,000 active duty soldiers, 789,000 reserve components, 39,000 reservists on active duty, and 412,000 civilians for a total Army strength of almost 2 million persons, the efficiency of a combat-to-noncombat ratio of about one to twenty-three under which the Army is currently organized to fight wars must be questioned.

Another pressing issue is the mental quality of U.S. Army soldiers. When compared with the quality of the mid- and late 1970s, today's quality recruit indeed shows much improvement. However, this improvement for the most part contrasts late 1970s' data from the bottom of the quality spectrum with current recruit data. Presently quality soldiers in the U.S. Army are defined as high school graduates often with a further note that a high percentage are above average within mental categories I to IIIA on the Armed Forces Qualification Test (AFQT). Table 3.1 makes clear the various strata involved in categorizing the U.S. population by mental capability.

It should be no surprise that the majority of quality recruits claimed by the Army today come from the middle one-third of the population, which is category III. The division of the middle third into categories IIIA and IIIB was done for marketing purposes to reflect a higher recruiting take of the above average or quality recruits. Ultimately, it is important not to be overly concerned about the U.S. Army definition of quality soldiers, but to ask whether the current Army definition of quality (i.e., high school graduate or top half in mental capability) is adequate in a competing strategies analysis to match the quality and performance of soldiers available to other armies. As was made apparent in the preceding chapter, the changing strategic environment will increasingly raise the question as to whether the highest-quality soldiers (top one-third) will defend the nation, as currently is the case in Israel, the U.S.S.R., and other armies, but not in the United States. Figure 3.1 makes clear that the U.S. Army does not significantly reflect the actual top quality (top one-third) of the American youth population, which is mostly college-bound.

What this figure makes evident is that of the approximately 9,360,000 American youths available in the seventeen- to twenty-one-year-old

TABLE 3.1
U.S. Population by Mental Capability

AFQT Category	Percent of U.S. Civilian Youth Population (17–21 years)
I	8
II	29
III	33
IV	21
V	9

Source: Population Representation Department of Defense, Asst. Secretary of Defense (Manpower, Installations and Logistics), June 1985.

- 17—21 YEAR OLD
- UPPER 50%

9.36M TOTAL MARKET
— 5.62M NOT QUALIFIED (INCLUDES QUALIFIED TSC IIIB & IV'S)
— 2.55M COLLEGE
— .39M IN SERVICE

800,000 AVAILABLE FY88

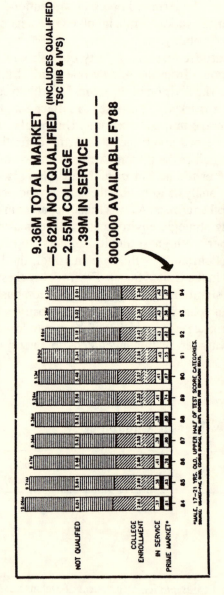

THE MARKET IS SHRINKING

- ALL SERVICES ARE COMPETING IN A SHRINKING PRIME MARKET

FIGURE 3.1 — Quality Male Market (*Source:* USAREC Briefing)

category each year, the Army is competing with the other armed services as well as industry for less than 10 percent of the available market, which in reality comes mostly from the middle one-third in quality. In unvarnished terms this means that the Army attempts each year to recruit its quality soldiers from the marginal population remaining in the market after the approximately 900,000 top-quality college freshmen have entered college. This leaves about 800,000 youth, primarily from the middle one-third in quality, in the market from which the Army must recruit about 75,000 each year in competition with industry and the other services. This youth pool, already marginal, will decline over the next several years for demographic reasons. The market is projected to decline to 670,000 in 1990 and 560,000 in 1993.

A more accurate perception of the quality actually achieved is indicated by the fact that even though well over 90 percent of each year's incoming recruits are high school graduates, the average reading level of today's Army is at about the tenth grade, only two grade levels above the eighth grade level of the "hollow Army" of the 1970s. Further, even though the Army is well over 90 percent high school graduates, over 100,000 soldiers enroll each year in the Army's Basic Skills Program in an effort to raise their reading, writing, and arithmetic skills to an acceptable level. While the entry scores of these recruits might compare favorably with the scores of those in the hollow Army of the 1970s, Table 3.2 makes clear that the U.S. Army could do much better in warfighting if the potential performance of the top one-third indicated in the table were available to Army combat units.

Nevertheless, since the early 1980s the Army has been marketing the notion that quality soldiers, as defined by the Army, are the answer to its warfighting manpower problems. Marked success in recruiting quality soldiers from 1981 onward alleviated many discipline and performance problems associated with the hollow Army of the late 1970s. However, the real question is how much improvement in the manpower, personnel, and training areas has been made in the Army over the past ten to fifteen years, and what is the significance of these improvements in the context of competing strategies. Is this Army about to enter the 1990 era indeed "the best Army in the world," as recently proclaimed?[9] Unfortunately, considerable data exist (Chapters 4 to 8) to indicate today's Army is only average to mediocre in the vital areas of manpower, unit leadership, cohesion, and sustained training and performance. What has been achieved since the early 1980s and through the end of the decade is to raise an Army that had fallen to the lowest standards of performance, one that had almost unravelled and was on the ropes, up to current midrange

TABLE 3.2
Relationship of AFQT to Other Measures

AFQT CAT	AFQT PERCENTILE	GENERAL TECHNICAL	READING GRADE LEVEL	LEVEL OF TRAINABILITY	
I	93-99	130-155	12.7-12.9	WELL ABOVE AVERAGE	⎱ TOP
II	64-92	110-129	10.6-12.6	ABOVE AVERAGE	⎰ 1/3
IIIA	50-63	100-109	9.3-10.5	AVERAGE	
IIIB	31-49	90-99	8.1-9.2	AVERAGE	
IV	10-30	75-89	6.6-8.0	BELOW AVERAGE	
V	0-9	52-74	3.4-6.5	WELL BELOW AVERAGE	

Source: USAREC Briefing

standards of performance. A stable, nonstressful international environment over the past decade and a half kept the Army well away from any significant deployment or other source of stress and allowed the Army to rebuild. But, to date, the standards of unit performance achieved cast doubts on the claim that today's Army is the "best ever." An objective view of the data suggests the Army must progress much further if it is to achieve status as a first-rate army capable of holding its own worldwide.

Improvements in discipline indicators over the past several years have been based almost completely upon the recruitment of higher-quality soldiers. However, the related expectations of vastly improved unit performance, also based on projections of higher-quality soldiers, have not been realized. Inflated claims notwithstanding, today's Army as currently organized has reached its limits and is not continuing to improve in that area in most need of improvement, unit performance. The goal to date has been limited to recruiting quality soldiers. The goal should be quality *units*. Except for measurements in several areas of discipline indicators (e.g., theft, absent without leave [AWOL], etc.), and higher individual test scores, measures of unit performance remain remarkable for their average and mediocre nature. Further, the improved individual behavior scores on discipline and potential for individual performance are primarily because of the values and traits present when the individual recruits enter the Army. The Army has marketed these inherited personal characteristics and the resulting improved behavior statistics of its new quality soldiers but has failed to translate them into consistently high-performing units. Instead, units continue to have great difficulty in sustaining above-average standards of performance. The failure to translate improved individual soldier potential into higher levels of unit performance necessary to win is attributable to several factors. Chapters 4 through 8 discuss related organizational, leadership, and training factors. The remainder of this chapter examines the much-touted improvement in warfighting capability attributed to improved soldier quality and concludes that this improved warfighting capability has been marketed to such an extent that the message and conclusion presently being promoted are not accurate reflections of the U.S. Army's warfighting capability. This is not only misleading; it is dangerous.

When the manpower substance of the Army is examined it becomes clear that perhaps the glass is more than half empty. While the marketeers have been presenting the "glass is half full" message no one has looked at the glass half empty in a comprehensive manner. This chapter outlines the manpower issues involved. First, the well-marketed increase in numbers of quality soldiers will have little significant impact on Army warfighting capability. From the lowest point of the hollow Army in 1980 to 1987, the Army approximately doubled its yearly take of top-quality (category I and II) recruits. However, beginning early in 1987, the Army began a slow but continuous decline in the numbers of quality soldiers enlisted. This decline has continued and has resulted in the percentage of category IV soldiers (bottom one-third) increasing from 4 percent to about 8 percent in 1989.[10] Even going back to its best years for quality recruits, 1986 and 1987, the results were not significant. During these two best-case years the Army increased its annual total of top-quality recruits by an average of 21,000 per year over the early 1980s. However, an attrition rate of about 35 percent (actually higher for top-quality soldiers) means that over 7,000 of these soldiers will not complete their contracted service. Of the approximately 14,000 remaining, relatively few serve in the infantry, armor, or artillery. For example, the net annual increase in top-quality soldiers (category I and II) for the entire armor branch over the numbers experienced during the hollow Army era is only about 600 soldiers. This is a strategically insignificant number in the context of competing strategies, hardly capable of raising the Army's warfighting capability even if the Army were able to successfully translate the potential of quality soldiers into sustained higher unit performance, an outcome the Army has failed to accomplish to date. With the recent downturn in recruiting quality soldiers these data will become more worrisome.

Even more discouraging is the realization that because of assignment policies and low reenlistments among high-quality soldiers, few of these soldiers make their way into the NCO ranks of the infantry, armor, or artillery. For example, data reflecting a high point of quality recruiting show a total of only 396 top-quality (category I and II) staff sergeants (E-6) in military occupational specialty (MOS) 19K (M-1 tank) in the entire Army. This is 26 percent of the total (1,495) of 19K staff sergeants in the Army. This means that at any one time for this critical MOS of tank commanders for the M-1 Abrams tank, that the Army has approximately one-half of this number, or about 200 (13 percent) top-quality M-1 tank commanders actually serving in armor units. In the next grade down with a total of about 611 (25 percent) top-quality 19K sergeants E-5 the problem is proportionately the same with about 300, or 12 percent, serving with armor units.[11] These percentages will not improve as more M60 tank staff sergeants make the transition into the newer M-1 tank. Only 25 percent (371) of the M60 tank commanders are in the top one-third with about 12 percent, or 185, top one-third staff sergeants actually serving in M60 armor units. The percentages are even lower in the infantry, with about 13 percent of the staff sergeants actually serving as infantry squad leaders in the top one-third and about 11 percent of Bradley fighting vehicles commanders in the top one-third. In view of these considerations and with similar data available for all of the trigger-pulling branches, it is not unreasonable to conclude that the new quality Army is having a minimal impact on the Army's direct warfighting capability.

In addition to claims of improved numbers of quality soldiers, related Army claims of improved performance should be examined closely in order to determine if the quality being achieved is comparable to the quality soldiers present in other armies. When properly organized and led, smart soldiers do much better. Within the past several years research has been able to demonstrate what some commanders have known intuitively for years. Reliable data are available through the Army's research Project A and other sources that are able to correlate soldier performance with mental category for many military occupational specialties in the U.S. Army, especially for the combat arms.[12] Figure 3.2 indicates the significance of this kind of data for combat performance. Table 3.3 distinguishes the performance of top one-third soldiers and relates the tremendous combat potential associated with the top mental categories.

Similar performance data will also allow analysts to compare combat performance among the major armies of the world. While data comparable to Project A data are not readily available for most other armies, such data from the U.S. Army make the projections for expected combat performance of other armies much easier to forecast. If we know the manpower defense policies, specifically the draft, classification, assignment, and leadership practices of specific armies, we can say much about the soldier combat performance capabilities of these armies. For example, we know, in broad terms, enough about the manpower policies of Soviet, Israeli, and other armies to be able to forecast the mental capabilities of combat soldiers in these armies, where the smart soldiers are assigned and approximately in what numbers. We know, for example, that the Israelis have multiplied their warfighting capability tremendously through assigning the highest-quality people available in Israeli society to combat units and especially to leadership positions in small combat units.[13] We know the reverse is true of other armies in the Middle East and expect the results of these MPT policies to be reflected in warfighting.

When applied to the U.S. Army, this comparative approach shows cause for concern. Most of the high quality recently achieved is actually

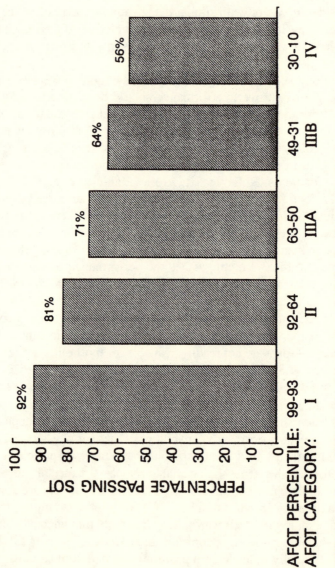

FIGURE 3.2 — Soldier Performance on Skill Qualification Tests by Mental Category (*Source*: The Army's Quality Need: Manpower and Personnel Lab: Army Research Institute: Unpublished briefing charts.)

TABLE 3.3
Air Defense Artillery Ranging Proficiency (All Actions Correct)
Armed Forces Qualification Test Score Category

AFQT SCORE CATEGORY		REDEYE		STINGER	
		ALL ACTIONS CORRECT (%)	% INCREASE RELATIVE TO CATEGORY IV	ALL ACTIONS CORRECT (%)	% INCREASE RELATIVE TO CATEGORY IV
TOP 1/3	I	58.3	59%	76.7	48%
	II	57.0	56%	67.3	30%
MIDDLE 1/3	IIIA	51.3	40%	61.4	19%
	IIIB	44.3	21%	56.4	9%
LOWER 1/3	IV	36.6	--	51.8	--

Source: DA Briefing

just about average, as Figure 3.2 indicates. Additionally, when matched against the strategic requirement cited in the preceding chapter, the limited numbers involved in actual increased quality are strategically insignificant. Further, following chapters show that the limited quality the U.S. Army has achieved is not, for the most part, assigned to combat units to directly enhance warfighting capabilities and that significant pockets of mediocrity and less than optimum unit performance will continue to exist indefinitely under current organization and policies. Recruiting quality soldiers, to date, has not significantly improved the Army's overall warfighting capability beyond midrange levels of unit performance. If the overall manpower situation is considered rather than allowing overstated and carefully selected and marketed manpower data to define the issue, it becomes clear the Army has not yet benefited from improved quality in unit performance. Quality units, not quality soldiers, should be the final goal.

In continuing an examination of the glass half empty, Table 3.4 reflects the actual reasons why recruits joined the Army during the period of its most successful recruitment of quality recruits. It makes clear that the primary motivation to join is based on an individual calculation of economic gain or personal advantage. This "economic man" motivation appears to be unchanged since the start of the all-volunteer Army.[14]

An in-depth article on Army recruits in the *Washington Post* appears to sum up these reasons for joining. The headline reads: "Among Today's Recruits, U.S. Military Is Viewed As Their Step Upward."[15] Unfortunately, the economic man motivation, which appears to be the prime mover in attracting recruits into the Army, continues to persist once the recruit is in the Army. In first-rate armies, it doesn't matter what motivation brings a man into the army. Whether recruits join for

TABLE 3.4
Reason for Enlistment Recruits: High School Graduates, Top Half Mental Category
n = 6,885

Economic or Personal Gain	89%
Serve Country	9%
Other	2%
	100% Total

economic reasons, the draft, or varied motivations, as in the French foreign legion, the unit should envelope soldiers and gain their primary commitment. Other than for a brief period for most recruits during basic training, the U.S. Army fails to sustain the commitment to unit that is characteristic of a great army. The continual long-term decrease in soldier commitment to unit and Army values that occurs from the relative high reached by soldiers in basic training (see Chapter 7) is a strong indication that the Army has not developed strong units with well-integrated long-term soldier-leader relationships. Instead the Army has drifted into an organizational mode characterized by leadership and personnel procedures that result in nascent or turbulent organization at the troop level, which makes the development and sustainment of strong, well-led units very difficult.

In concrete terms this has led to continuing dismal attrition statistics in addition to discouraging data on soldiers' professional motivation and their commitment to their immediate units and leaders. Attrition rates of between 30 and 40 percent in many military occupational specialties, including the combat arms, currently being experienced by the U.S. Army are unheard of for any army that aspires to the status of a great army. Such attrition reflects a real softness in soldier commitment and the failure of the COHORT program. In terms of Moskos' institutional-occupational dichotomy,[16] such attrition is an indicator that in large part the U.S. soldier is just filling another job into which he was attracted by economic considerations, in which he is sustained by economic motivation, and from which he can quit, as many are doing.

Attrition data from the early 1980s onward have not changed significantly from the current high rates. The current attrition rate for the overall active Army is about 35 percent. This means that 35 percent of the soldiers recruited in any one year will depart the Army prior to completing the term called for in their contracts.[17] For example, if the Army enlists 120,000 recruits during a typical year, about 42,000 of this number will leave before their contracts are completed. These soldiers leave primarily as a result of their decision to quit and resulting actions or behavior that lead to discharge. As indicated elsewhere, four out of the five top reasons for leaving the Army included poor small-unit leadership as the primary factor.[18] If Army-initiated attrition is also included, such as early outs, total attrition reaches about 40 percent. Such statistics indicate that quitting the Army is reasonably easy and painless, as "bad paper" or other sanctions for failure to meet obligations are very infrequent. Even more discouraging are the attrition rates among combat arms soldiers in infantry, armor, and artillery who joined at the height of the Army's success in the middle 1980s in attracting quality recruits. Attrition rates for these combat soldiers are over 35 percent with some combat MOS (e.g., 19K) sometimes over 40 percent. Soldiers with strong commitments to their units and strong professional values do not leave at these rates.

There is some indication that those who do not leave remain to protect accrued benefits such as their college fund. Certainly reenlistment rates especially among quality top one-third first-term soldiers do not augur well for the future small-unit leadership of the Army. The top one-third quality soldiers the Army needs, especially those in the combat arms, are reenlisting in very small numbers. Small-unit leadership needs in the combat arms projected in Chapter 6 cannot be met or even approached at current reenlistment rates. The few hundred top-quality soldiers who finish their first term each year and reenlist into infantry, armor, and artillery units fall far short of meeting the leadership needs of these units.

The impact on warfighting of inadequate numbers of combat troops; persistent economic man motivation; high attrition rates; low reenlistment rates of top one-third first-term soldiers; and low soldier commitment to unit, leaders, and professional values would be severe in the event of war. Unlike readiness reports in other armies and even in the U.S. Air Force, U.S. Army readiness reports do not reflect these factors. Instead such assessments are left to the judgment of the commander. Two considerations make such subjective readiness evaluations unreliable. One is the natural human tendency to evaluate the results of personal effort positively, especially when the individuals involved are achievement-oriented, as are U.S. Army commanders. The results of such evaluations can be misleading, as evidenced by data presented later that show that over 90 percent of U.S. Army company grade officers believe their personal performance puts them among the top 20 percent in performance. This attitude is present at all levels and is reinforced by our efficiency report system with its tendency to rate most officers as far above average. More importantly, the second factor influencing the unreliable and overoptimistic readiness reports is the tremendous pressure on the commander to submit "can do" reports. As long as the system hides behind the judgment call of the commander, the assumptions on which force structure, organization, and budgets are presently based will continue to reflect commanders' contrived and overly optimistic readiness reports. If commanders were to give accurate reports on the state of unit training, manpower, support, and so on, the assumptions upon which the entire force structure of the Army rests would come under profound questioning.

Further, in many feasible warfighting scenarios the U.S. Army could quickly find itself facing again a situation similar to that faced in the early 1970s. The question could again become: "Will they fight?" In responding to this question the bluster of unit commanders should be avoided. Recent experience in Vietnam supports the view that units without strong commitment and cohesion around strong professional norms are open to outside or distracting societal influences that affect the behavior of soldiers and unit performance. Given another unpopular, politically divisive war that lasts beyond several weeks, with high casualties spread unevenly through the population, it is likely that many of today's first-term soldiers will seriously reconsider their willingness to remain in the Army. In other words, they will not fight in these circumstances, at least not with the skill and commitment necessary to win.

The reserve components, the Army Reserve and the Army National Guard, cannot provide the answer to the Army's manpower problems. In fact, when the U.S. Army reserve components are included in the manpower equation the overall problems become more burdensome. Even when the generally accepted number of 780,000 reservists are included, the Army's limited capability to mass combat soldiers is not significantly improved. The recognized need is for over 1.2 million reservists but the number has currently been limited to 780,000 in an attempt to make the problems of modernizing the reserve components more manageable.[19] The combat units available through the reserves add only 35,000 (approximately) trigger-pulling troops to the 50,000 active duty combat troops in units for a total Army capability of about 85,000 troops. For a number of scenarios that could call for U.S. Army involvement even under a reduced one-and-a-half-war strategy, the present overall reserve capability is strategically insignificant. Under a comparative competing strategies approach, for example, the Soviets have an overall available manpower pool of 5.5 million reservists. Because the Soviets draft about 900,000 men every six months, they have an immense and immediate pool of 9 million reservists who have served in the past five years. This is far more than the 2 million reservists the Soviets require to meet their immediate wartime needs.[20] It is unclear at this point what effects a recent decision to defer some Soviet college students will have on the Soviet armed forces over time.

Closer examination of U.S. Army reserves make clear that additional major problems exist beyond the very small number of combat troops available from the reserve components. The reserve force structure problem is complicated by the decision several years ago to "round out" understrength active Army units by filling their personnel vacancies with reserve and National Guard units. This has been done to the extent that presently over 40 percent of all forces necessary during the first thirty days of war would come from the reserve components. In fact, most of these reserve units would be deployed before many active duty units. By all accounts, including congressional testimony, these forces are not capable of meeting their missions. According to one high-ranking officer, "Roundout is not working. These forces will not be prepared to go to war ... the Army is deceiving itself to state otherwise ... our Service is choking on our reserve components."[21]

The "total force" concept calls for active duty forces to become smaller while allowing newly modernized reserve forces to fill in or round out active forces, for example, by designating one brigade out of three in a division a reserve brigade. It was thought that the economies achieved through the use of less expensive reserve forces would make the strategic risks involved acceptable. However, congressional testimony and other sources make clear that this approach is not working. So much of the active force today (40 percent) is dependent on the reserves that active Army units could not fight without them during the first thirty days of war in Europe.[22] However, closed congressional testimony by Army Reserve, National Guard, and General Accounting Office witnesses made clear that these reserve units cannot meet the requirements necessary to support a war in Europe. One senator summed up the testimony by stating: "We just couldn't fight"; this lack of support is a major factor in General Bernard Rogers' (ret.) view as a former supreme commander of NATO forces that NATO would have to use nuclear weapons within two weeks of the start of a war in Europe.[23]

In view of immediate wartime missions assigned these reserve units to fill out active duty units and the significant shortcomings involved, the question arises if these units can be called reserves at all. Instead it might be more realistic to consider these units as active units in deep hibernation with significant personnel and training problems.

In addition to the severe shortage in numbers of combat troops available in the reserves, there are also significant problems in quality, training, and internal organization such as attrition and turbulence. These become major factors affecting U.S. Army warfighting capability when considered through a competing strategies approach that compares our reserves with the capabilities of other nations such as the Israelis, the West Germans, or the Soviets.

The quality of reserve forces is a major consideration in comparing value added to a nation's warfighting ability by its reserve forces.

Without extensively reviewing much material covered elsewhere it is sufficient to state that the quality of the reserve components generally reflects the quality of the active Army with perhaps somewhat more favorable but insignificant numbers when it is realized that the Soviets have millions of reservists at a higher level of readiness and training at the category I and II mental levels. This is true also of the West German and Israeli reserve forces, which in the case of Israel have been the primary force in the repeated Israeli victories in the Middle East.

In any U.S. attempt to prepare rapidly for war the fact that we cannot readily draw on adequate numbers of top-quality reservists would become a major limitation in U.S. warfighting ability. Table 3.5 makes clear the significance of high-quality reservists. For example, in only four training attempts 80 percent of the top-quality soldiers (categories I–II) were able to fire a missile successfully while only 42 percent of the middle-quality soldiers (category III) and 4 percent of the bottom-quality soldiers (category IV) were able successfully to do the job. For a nation in a mobilization crisis, attempting to bring its warfighting potential to bear rapidly, it is imperative that its soldiers are of the highest capability possible. Weeks and months could be added to mobilization by the need to train less than top-quality soldiers. This criterion is not presently being met in today's reserve components. Except for the generally well qualified officers and some noncommissioned officers, today's reserve components are comprised largely of lower- and middle-category personnel. This should not be surprising because this is also true in active Army units where there are also insignificant numbers of top-quality soldiers from which the reserve components can draw, especially in the combat branches.

The significance of quality for soldier and unit performance in war is immense. A recent U.S. Army Recruiting Command report on the benefits of quality soldiers stated that when the highest-quality (category I) soldiers were in key tank crew positions in a European scenario, they achieved a tank kill ratio of 7.45 to 1 over lower-quality soldiers (category IV) in similar positions.[24]

In summary Table 3.5 suggests that we should expect average and below average performance from our reserve components when compared to the reserve capabilities of other nations, which have significant portions of their reserve forces comprised of top-third soldiers.

Just as it is with active duty forces, sustaining levels of training in the reserve components to ensure reliable standards of performance is an enormous problem and one that is a major factor in preventing reserve

TABLE 3.5
Low-Aptitude Personnel Require at Least Double Training Time and Help

MISSILE TASK: CUMULATIVE PERCENTAGE OF SOLDIERS REACHING CRITERION PER TRIAL

CUM % REACHING TRIAL	2	3	4	5	6	7	8	9	10	11	12	13	14	15
TSC I-II	30	65	80	94	94	100								
TSC III	8	14	42	70	74	92	100							
TSC IV			4	14	14	28	38	42	48	57	66	71	76	76

FOR MISSILE TASK LOW APTITUDE GROUP REQUIRED:

- THREE TIMES MORE PROMPTS THAN MID-APTITUDE GROUP
- TWICE AS MANY TRIALS
- OVER TWICE THE TIME

Source: TRADOC Briefing

units from currently meeting their commitments in Europe and elsewhere in time of war. Summarized briefly, the problem is that the average of forty-one days that the reserve soldier actually spends each year with his unit is not adequate for the soldier to reach and maintain levels of skill proficiency necessary for units to enter combat.[25] Such critical skilled personnel as tank turret mechanics, tank commanders, and gunners are not available in the numbers and degree of proficiency required. Even if there were enough high-quality personnel available, the limited number of training days and the complexity of the technology involved ensure that "skill decay," or the rate at which soldiers lose their skills, will preclude these units from reaching the necessary standards of performance in the time allotted. Figure 3.3 indicates the frequency of practice necessary in just one infantry skill if minimal warfighting skills of performance are to be maintained.

In the critical armor crewman skills the sustainment of training is much more difficult. Figure 3.4 hints at the magnitude of the task by demonstrating the training necessary just to maintain one relatively simple

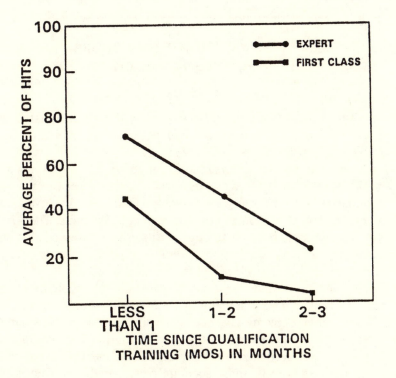

FIGURE 3.3 — Infantry Antitank Firing Performance

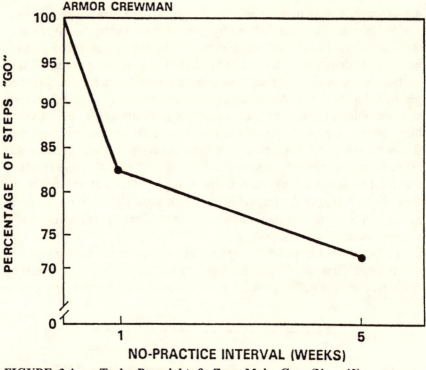

FIGURE 3.4 — Task: Boresight & Zero Main Gun (N = 42)

task out of the hundreds necessary to be performed if a tank and its crew are to be able to reach and sustain top performance standards in a reasonable amount of time upon mobilization.

It is clear that the present system of limited weekend meetings and two weeks' training per year cannot meet and sustain the necessary levels of performance in order for the reserve components to be full partners in the total Army round out strategy of augmenting active units. The Army needs to adopt a rapid train-up strategy for its critical reserve skills and allow enough time in its strategic calculations to allow these reserve forces to reach the necessary levels of proficiency.

Finally, the many and significant organizational problems of the reserve components present a major obstacle to U.S. Army warfighting capabilities. These problems have been extensively outlined elsewhere.[26] The effects of two of these organizational problems on Army warfighting capabilities must be recognized if the reserve component contribution to actual warfighting is to be more accurately estimated. The first is the extremely high attrition rate in reserve component units. Chapters 4 and 5 make clear the effects of attrition on unit performance and reserve units suffer unusually high attrition. At the sergeant (E-5) and lower levels, annual attrition has been conservatively estimated to average at least 50 percent.[27] Unit performance problems outlined for active units suffering from attrition and related effects are even more pronounced in reserve units, especially those round out units scheduled to deploy within hours and days of notification. The lack of training and cohesion in such units is especially serious in view of the fact that these units represent a large portion of the Army's very limited ability to mass combat troops and over one-third of its infantry forces. We should not expect these units to perform at the level of reserve units in other armies where quality is higher and attrition rates much lower. The unwritten but widely recognized option of quitting the U.S. Army without sanction, now evident in the active Army, is also rampant in reserve units. Contrasted with the ease with which U.S. soldiers can quit or change their occupations, Soviet soldiers including reservists are immersed in a service ethic and bound closely to their units for the duration of their active and reserve service.[28]

The second problem, which we should expect to be a far greater problem for our Army than for others, is the expected "show rate" among the reserve components in the event of war. Given the unprecedented role of reserve components in our immediate defense plans, the question of how many reservists will report to their units or station on the designated day is very significant. Current assumptions about who will show up for the next war are based on dated interpretations of reserve call-ups in World War II, the Korean War, and the Berlin Crisis. There are presently no valid show rate data about what to expect today. Recent attempts to pay a few preselected individual ready reservists to show for one day cannot be considered a valid measurement of reserve show rates.

Currently military planners are assuming a 100 percent show rate for all soldiers in selected reserve units, especially those slated to immediately round out active units in the event of war. Even this assumption for these selected reserve units must be questioned. In reserve units recently selected to attend the National Training Center in Ft. Irwin attrition increased by an average of about 20 percent over normal.[29] On this basis an assumed show rate of 100 percent for reserve units in the event of war is questionable, especially in view of the occupational ethos and its option of "quitting a job" that most present-day reservists were exposed to in the active Army.

The problems faced in another element of the reserve components, the Individual Ready Reserve (IRR), are far more overwhelming and serious for the total Army concept. The IRR is slated for a wartime mission that it, in all probability, cannot meet. Briefly stated the role of the IRR is to provide the hundreds of thousands of individual soldiers by MOS that wartime units will need as "fillers," especially during the first weeks and months of war. For example, it is estimated that during the first thirty days of war about 100,000 replacements will be required to replace casualties alone and the IRR is expected to shoulder much of this burden in addition to providing fillers for the initial deployment of units at the start of such a war. It must be noted that the latter requirement is enormous in itself. The Vice Chief of Staff of the U.S. Army, at the time General Thurman, acknowledged that the active Army required at least 125,000 additional troops to fill it out for warfighting.[30] This estimate was given prior to the most recent force structure cut of 10,000 soldiers in 1988 and further cuts announced in 1989.

It is evident the task facing the IRR is enormous. It should also be evident that the IRR as currently organized and managed cannot meet the task. Estimates of the size of the IRR vary from 290,000 to about 450,000 soldiers.[31] The big question about these soldiers is how many will be available when needed. Currently there is no accepted and valid show rate for the IRR. Even with all the organizational hedging imaginable, the Army acknowledges that about 40 percent of the IRR cannot be found. The Army does not know where they are and does not have the ability to contact them. This figure is based on an assumed IRR strength of only 290,000. If the strength of 450,000 is used instead, the Army is unable presently to locate well over 50 percent of the IRR. The numbers are made manageable and less alarming by the practice of arbitrarily dropping soldiers from the IRR when they have gone unlocated for a period of time.

In sum there is a major discrepancy between the strategists and planners who assume the IRR can and will perform its wartime tasks and the many indicators that the IRR in fact cannot perform as expected. Almost completely ignored is that notification procedures for members of the IRR are very unreliable. As mentioned, the Army is unable even to locate many soldiers in the IRR. Additionally, the Army lacks vital and current information on the family and medical situations of IRR reservists. More important, the Army has no working knowledge about the amount of training necessary to bring these soldiers even to minimal skill levels. Finally, just as with selected reserve units, the Army has no valid or reliable information about show rates for members of the IRR that can be found. Forgotten is the fact that most soldiers were placed in the IRR because they originally opted to quit or were fired from their original reserve units. In many cases, the assumption is doubtful that IRR members will willingly reenter a reserve unit, especially one called to active duty. In terms of a competing strategies approach, the state of the U.S. IRR becomes especially significant when it is recognized that the Soviet Army reliably has at its fingertips millions of soldiers in its organizational equivalent of the IRR.

The limitations of a Total Army concept that places so much burden and responsibility on its reserve components must be recognized. Our reserve components must either be improved or our expectations must be lowered. We must experience a *glasnost* of our own and acknowledge that as currently organized and managed the reserve components contribute little actual strength in many likely scenarios to U.S. Army ability to mass combat troops; those troops that are available should not be considered reserves in the traditional sense but poorly trained soldiers in deep hibernation that are dedicated to active duty Army missions; and that the lower-ranking soldiers and NCOs are, for the most part, drawn from the middle and bottom third of the population in terms of quality and resulting performance. Further, the United States has no system to ensure that the top one-third of its citizens in terms of capability and performance are available to the services through a reserve system with capabilities similar to those of world-class armies such as the Soviet or Israeli armies. Finally, inadequate training, rapid skill decay, no strategy or system for rapid reserve component training in time of war, significant attrition rates, and the questionable capability of the IRR in the event of war all point to the need for a major and open reassessment of Total Army warfighting capabilities.

Many overall problems could be relieved through additional manpower while others could be relieved through organizational change and new policy. As noted earlier, wisdom often involves recognition of what can be changed and what cannot be changed. In this regard it is almost axiomatic that the Army cannot presently expect additional manpower or dollars to improve its warfighting capability. Any change or improvement has to be accomplished with the resources on hand and it is here that significant improvement can be made.

NOTES

1. Carl Von Clausewitz, *On War*, trans. Michael Howard and Peter Parent (Princeton, N.J.: Princeton University Press, 1976), 195.

2. *FM 100-5 Operations* (Washington, D.C.: U.S. Army, 1982), B-2.

3. Ibid., 1–2.

4. Clausewitz, *On War*, 184–89, 282–84.

5. Ibid., 285–91.

6. Letter to Deputy Chief of Staff for Personnel from Commanding General, Forces Command, Subject: U.S. Army Manning System Concept, July 14, 1983.

7. Kenneth C. Leuer, "More Boots on Ground," *Army Times*, March 14, 1988, 10.

8. Totals for combat troops are based on strength reports and personal inquiries. Actual totals are probably smaller because totals in text are high-sided on the side of overestimating the actual numbers of combat troops available for massing.

9. Delbert L. Spurlock, "On the Record," *Army Times*, October 17, 1988, 22.

10. Jim Tice, "Reenlistments Ease the Pain of Bearish Recruiting Market," *Army Times*, April 17, 1989, 6. The insignificance of the quality achieved is evident in the increase in armor of about 600 annually as explained further on in the text. This number is based on an annual recruiting goal for the armor branch of approximately 3,700 with an average top-quality percentage of recruits of about one-third compared to a top-quality percentage of about one-sixth in 1980.

11. Army Personnel Master File, Total Army Personnel Agency (TAPA), Alexandria, Va., May 1988. The numbers of top one-third NCOs actually serving in units was determined through discussion with TAPA personnel and through sampling. The percentages were safe-sided to err on the high side.

12. Francis C. Crafton, Darlene M. Olson, Newell Kent Eaton, and Laurence M. Hanser, *Project A Concurrent Validation Results* and Briefing "The Army's Project A — Improving Selection, Classification and Utilization of Army Enlisted Personnel," (Alexandria, Va.: Army Research Institute, 1987). Project A is a comprehensive, long-range research and development program undertaken by the U.S. Army to improve soldier effectiveness by matching personnel requirements with those soldiers most capable of performing well, as determined through entry-level selection and classification tests. Combat performance appears to be influenced by other factors as well as mental capability. S. L. A. Marshall in *Men Against Fire* observed that in the U.S. Army in World War II very few infantrymen fired their weapons at the enemy. Later research by David Rowland, "Assessment of Combat Degradation," *The Quarterly Journal*, RUSI (June 1986) suggests that fewer than 20 percent of riflemen inflicted an average of four casualties each, with the remaining riflemen inflicting none. Historical analysis by Peter W. Kuzumplich in *Comparative Wartime Replacement Systems* (Washington, D.C.: Defense Intelligence Agency, 1986) suggests that the low volume of fire observed in World War II was, in part, attributable to the lack of cohesion in U.S. units. He also reminds us that U.S. infantry units in World War II were not comprised of higher mental category soldiers. In this regard, more recent research in the United States (Project A) and abroad (e.g., Israel) strongly points to the positive effects on combat performance associated with higher mental category soldiers. Therefore, two major factors, low mental capability and low cohesion, appear to have had major effects on the performance of U.S. infantrymen in World War II.

13. Revben Gal, *The Israeli Soldier* (Westport, Conn.: Greenwood Press, 1987).

14. Franklin D. Margiotta et al., *Changing Military Manpower Realities* (Boulder, Colo.: Westview Press, 1983), 10.

15.   George C. Wilson, *Washington Post*, August 30, 1987, p. A10.

16.   Charles C. Moskos and Frank R. Wood, eds., *The Military — More Than Just a Job?* (New York: Pergamon-Brassey's, 1988).

17.   Army Personnel Master File.

18.   Army Exit Interviews in Issues Briefing for DCSPER, U.S. Army, May 27, 1986.

19.   Chief Reserve Components Training Strategy Task Force, Chamberlain Hotel, Fort Monroe, Va., October 21, 1987.

20.   John A. Goldsmith, "Manpower: A Weak Link?" *Military Logistics Forum*, April 1987, 32.

21.   Vernon A. Guidry, Jr., "Memo by General Says Army's Wartime Reserve Plan Won't Work," *Baltimore Sun*, September 16, 1986, 1.

22.   Joseph Golioto, "Organizational Culture and Readiness in the Reserve Components," Research Directorate, National Defense University, Ft. McNair, Washington, D.C., 1986, 3.

23.   George C. Wilson, "U.S. Reserves Called Insufficient for War in Europe," *Washington Post*, April 14, 1988, 9.

24.   Juri Toomipuu, "Cost and Benefits of Quality Soldiers," USARECRN 86-1, Army Recruiting Command, Ft. Sheridan, Ill., September 1986, 7.

25.   Reserve Component Training Task Force, In Progress Review (IPR), No. 5, January 1988.

26.   In addition to widespread and continuing commentary from a variety of civilian sources including the Congress and media, the Army periodically reviews reserve component problems in a long series of reports over the years. The latest such effort (1988–1989) is the Reserve Component Training Strategy Task Force based at TRADOC Headquarters.

27.   Reserve Component Task Force.

28.   William Darryl Henderson, *Cohesion: The Human Element in Combat* (Washington, D.C.: National Defense University Press, 1985), 41–44.

29.   Glenda Nogami, unpublished Army Research Institute report on attrition in the reserve components, 1988.

30.   Benjamin F. Schemmer, "Army Planning Revealed at Its Worst," *Armed Forces Journal*, April 1987, 14.

31.   Paul Babiak, "On the Record," *Army Times*, May 30, 1988, 22.

4

TRAINING ON A TREADMILL

In runners' terms the U.S. Army has "hit the wall" in its pursuit of highly trained, high-performing units. Invisible system barriers are keeping U.S. units on a training treadmill, never allowing most of them to rise above marginal performance in their ability to match the performance of the world's best armies.

The manpower and personnel factors that, in effect, have raised invisible barriers to effective unit training include:

- Training is not cumulative for U.S. units; rather it is "event driven" and short term.
- Performance at the National Training Center (NTC) measured over several years does not indicate the U.S. Army can compete successfully with world-class armies.
- Most units do not appear to be able to reach and sustain standards of performance above average to mediocre levels.
- The inability to sustain above-average unit performance indicates that manpower and personnel issues/policies are having significant effects on training and warfighting ability.
- Turbulence persists at high levels. The COHORT program, designed to reduce personnel turbulence and provide cohesion, is ineffective and cohesive units are not in evidence.
- The Enlisted Personnel Management System (EPMS) has muddied the traditional function of the NCO Corps and permitted the most qualified NCOs to separate themselves from soldiers.
- Quality small-unit leaders are not available in the necessary numbers to ensure effective training and high levels of unit performance.

- Personnel turbulence, small-unit leadership, and related enlisted personnel management issues are erecting major barriers to effective unit training and warfighting capability.

If the Army is to correct these significant shortfalls in unit training, we must be prepared to overcome current reluctance and follow the obvious beyond the training system and into the domain of the Army's personnel managers. It is here that the invisible wall has been erected that keeps most units on a training treadmill, struggling to maintain even mediocre performance and preventing them from breaking through to a level of excellence in unit performance. This was indirectly acknowledged by former Chief of Staff, General Wickham, at a farewell address to the Army's personnel community in March of 1987 when he stated in gentle terms that:

> The U.S. Army is not a great Army, just a good Army and the difference between a great Army and a good Army is leadership, leadership . . . in the units.[1]

That the former chief of staff said the Army was a "good" Army when he could as well have said it was "average" or, looking at the data, with justification even "mediocre," is not the point. The point is that he did not rank the U.S. Army as a great Army and he cited the primary reason as leadership. This conclusion by General Wickham is supported by the lessons learned form the NTC. Leadership at the small-unit level is not fully effective. This is reflected in unit performance, and much of the reason can be attributed to the personnel system.

The main problems with training in the U.S. Army do not rest with the subject matter, instructors, trainees, simulation, facilities, or curriculum priorities. In fact, great effort is made through the Army training system to ensure the overall but narrowly focused system is up to date and finely tuned. For example, an extensive and lengthy study was recently conducted on the content of basic training. It involved hundreds of people and was followed at the highest levels of the Army; the present Chief of Staff has declared himself to be the Army's top trainer. The study had little significant impact and like most other recent studies of Army training, it was not expected to have a major impact. Other than minor changes such as adjusting the number of minutes dedicated to bayonet training, little effect was noticed. The unspoken but recognized major assumption of this and other studies of the overall training system is that the training system is well designed and regulated, requiring only periodic fine tuning and necessary changes to incorporate the latest technology as it becomes available.

Yet, indicators are plentiful that U.S. Army units are not progressing and becoming more proficient. The system requires almost frenetic activity by commanders and soldiers in the short term to reach above-average levels of unit performance. But in the long term, in most cases, units just maintain average and in many cases marginal levels of unit performance. Certainly the system is not fully utilizing the tremendous potential available in the few quality soldiers now present in Army units.

Army training can be characterized as being event driven with units and their commanders (trainers) looking forward only to the next major event, for example, unit certification or the next rotation to the NTC. Short-term priorities dominate. Unit proficiency, professional knowledge, teamwork, and small-unit leadership do not grow and do not have a long-term cumulative effect on unit performance. Instead, there appears to be a series of short-term efforts to hold the system off, to hold assignments steady, and to train for an upcoming event (e.g., six months' preparation for the NTC) after which the short-term rules in effect during the preparation phase are relaxed, and the system reasserts itself with massively disruptive effects on any unit proficiency gained. The treadmill then continues with the commander rapidly refocusing on a new short-term event, with new people and new priorities.

The system factors affecting Army training are discernible and measurable but have been largely ignored. There is a basic and strong reluctance on the part of top leaders to examine critically a system in which they were professionally brought up and in which they were promoted, so they tend to accept it and maintain it on "their watch" largely as they found it. Nevertheless, evidence has been accumulating over the past several years that the current system is a structure with fragmented responsibilities and policies that is not capable of producing highly trained and high-performing units on a sustained basis. Yet, there is a curious, and in some cases a remarkably obstinate reluctance to follow obvious indicators of malfunction back to their root causes in the organization. Still, in many other cases, top leaders appear to be content in their assumption that the current system "is the best possible of all possible" systems.

The most accurate method of demonstrating that performance is not measuring up to necessary standards is to compare unit performance with the realistic but high standards necessary to compete with the performance of other world-class armies. Explaining the gap in Figure 4.1 between a measured level of performance and the standard of performance necessary to win wars is complex. However, as the figure

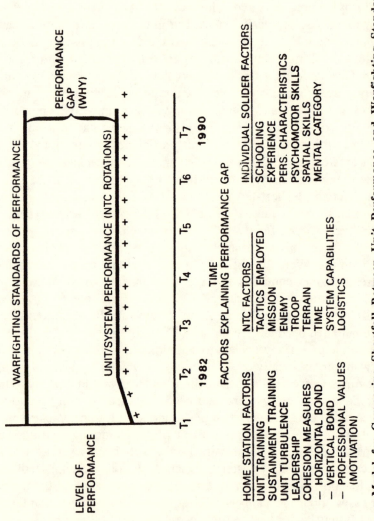

FIGURE 4.1 — Model for Comparing Shortfall Between Unit Performance and Warfighting Standards of Performance

indicates, major factors can be measured and their contribution or detraction to unit performance assessed.

This approach is especially well suited to measuring and assessing the factors behind unit performance at the Army's various combat training centers (CTC) of which the NTC is the most prominent.[2] The CTCs are designed to replicate battlefield conditions for unit training with the purpose of exposing combat units to intense and extended combat training and evaluate unit performance through diagnostic assessment of performance. The intent of the program is to allow combat units to train for the CTC, evaluate the unit's performance at the CTC, and then provide the unit with an extensive analysis and take-home package detailing their performance as the basis for subsequent unit training. In this manner, training benefits are supposed to accumulate. Unit knowledge, experience, teamwork, and proficiency all will grow and the unit will approach an apogee of combat readiness.

Unfortunately, this is not the case. At best, the CTCs train only individual leaders and staff, with those individual leaders and staff officers at battalion level receiving the most training. There is practically no long-term cumulative benefit for units, and reports indicate attendance at CTC is often a demotivator for the low-ranking soldier with no strong ties to his unit or immediate leader.

Evidence that training in the U.S. Army has stagnated on a long plateau of marginal unit performance with little long-term improvement is available from a number of sources. A 1986 report by the General Accounting Office on Army training concluded that the full potential of the NTC has not been realized because the Army failed to: "identify causes of Army-wide problems demonstrated during the center exercises and initiate solutions. Consequently, in 1985, units continued demonstrating problems in many of the same areas as they did in 1981."[3] This situation persists into 1990. The Army is not achieving a full return for the tremendous number of dollars spent on training. The NTC is a prime, if expensive, example of systemic failures in unit training throughout the Army. If the $385 million spent to develop the NTC is added to the total annual operating costs of $680 million since 1983, plus the conservative estimate of $600 million for the cost of over a hundred units attending the NTC since its beginning and the $42 million in instrumentation costs, the total cost of over $1.5 billion to date for the NTC is overwhelming, especially when the limited benefits are considered.

These costs should not detract from the tremendous potential of the unique training facility created by the Army at the National Training

Center. The NTC provides a place where a unit's training environment closely resembles that of actual combat. General Vuono, Chief of Staff of the Army, stated that the NTC provides "tough, realistic training . . . the best training in the Army today . . . units are gaining invaluable knowledge and experience that prepares them for war."[4] Unfortunately, the Army has not been able to demonstrate any meaningful gain or benefit for units at the NTC. At best, individual leaders might benefit but units experience little cumulative gain through their NTC experience. The long-term results and discouraging lack of any improvement in unit performance at the NTC over a recent five-year period is reflected in Figure 4.2.

The figure actually reflects two major points. First, over the period 1983 through 1987, unit performance at NTC was very stable with no improvement in unit performance. It is important to note that the unit performance indicated is for the period 1983–1987, during the Army's greatest success in attracting quality soldiers. The trend continued unchanged through 1988 and 1989. Second, the level of unit performance over time has been mediocre at best with only seventeen battalions out of almost a hundred able to win their battles during the six-year period. Even more discouraging is the fact that in performance measurements of the indicators (i.e., terrain domination and enemy/friendly casualties) of who wins and who loses in combat, the mean (approximately 50) U.S. score is well below the standard historically necessary (approximately 70) to be a winner on the battlefield.

When questioned on these results, the present institutional response tends to be that the opposing forces (OPFOR) at the NTC, modeled after the Soviet Army, are "over trained" and "better than the real" Soviet units the U.S. Army would face.[5] Such responses are little better than apologias and are belied by performance measurements that have little to do with OPFOR performance.

Without citing NTC performance measures that were hurriedly classified when the bad news they conveyed was finally realized, it is still possible to demonstrate unit performance far short of the standards necessary if the U.S. Army is to field high-performing units.

One of the strongest indicators of inadequate unit training are repeated failures to bring all of a unit's weapons to bear in a fight.[6] Over time at the NTC, 55 percent of the Army's most powerful weapons, the M-1 Abrams battle tanks, have not participated in or contributed to battle outcomes. Of the 45 percent of the M-1s that did fire during the many battles, the average range of engagement was between 1,357 meters and

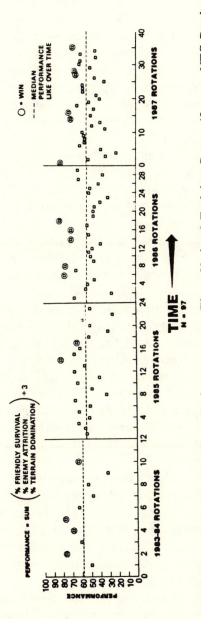
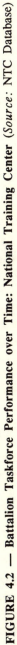

FIGURE 4.2 — Battalion Taskforce Performance over Time: National Training Center (*Source*: NTC Database)

1,520 meters, far short of their capability. The numbers are even worse for the less modern M-60 tanks, with 57 percent not participating.[7] The performance of the Improved TOW Vehicle (ITV) and the new M-2 Bradley fighting vehicle (BFV) for the infantry is even more discouraging. The crews of these vehicles are not exploiting their vast firepower and potential for influencing the battle. Only 11 percent of the ITVs fire during any battle (89 percent of the ITVs did not fight) and only 19 percent of the BFVs fired their TOW antitank weapon during the battle (81 percent did not fire TOWs during battle). The overall average was 8.4 percent of the available TOW antitank weapons brought to bear during battles at the NTC.[8]

The shortfall of small-unit leader initiative at NTC has been widely cited and illustrated by examples.[9] As noted, it is a major factor in the failure of the majority of M-1 tanks and Bradley fighting vehicles to engage in the battles at the NTC over the past several years. These data are supported by personal observations. For example, a tank platoon deployed at the NTC to defend a low-lying ridge offering an unobstructed view of several miles to the front has its right flank attacked. Each tank in the platoon is destroyed without firing a shot, piecemeal, over a 20-minute period from the flank by the OPFOR when each tank could have redeployed on its own initiative to offer more effective resistance. Another example reflecting the lack of small-unit initiative occurred with disastrous results during a unit road march at night under blackout conditions. A Bradley fighting vehicle in the middle of the march column broke down. All vehicles behind it came to a halt. The squad leader track commander of the broken-down vehicle watched the blackout lights of the vehicle in front disappear into the night. He remained in his vehicle along with all of the vehicle commanders behind him for over thirty minutes until the unit executive officer made his way forward on foot from the end of the column.

Needless to say the effects of this inadequate leadership on the night march and the unit's tactical disposition were potentially disastrous in the short term and debilitating in the long term. Repeated similar observations, such as failure to bore sight weapons properly and small-unit defensive dispositions that direct fire into friendly units less than 1,000 meters away, signal difficulties at ensuring an adequate basic standard of performance at small-unit levels.

Such data are symptomatic of widespread and significant unit training problems and not unique to these systems alone. The cause appears to be generic within units and generalizable to most NTC unit performance data. Most straightforward and open "lessons-learned" evaluations of unit performance at the NTC over the past several years have acknowledged below-par unit performance. As noted earlier, however, there remains a curious reluctance on the part of the Army's leadership to follow these obvious indicators back to the causes. This is essential if the U.S. Army is to begin to field highly trained, high-performing units, and especially if the $1.5 billion already sunk into the NTC and similar amounts for future combat training centers at Fort Chaffee, Arkansas, and Hohenfels, Germany, are to yield full value for the dollars spent.[10]

One of the most insightful lessons-learned documents to emerge from the National Training Center was produced as a result of observations over three years by the former chief observer/controller at the NTC.[11] Commenting on requisite training in order for units to perform well at the NTC, the former chief observer stated that it is "relatively easy" to train the battalion commander, his staff, and the company commanders to operate well. The difficult training necessary for performing well at the NTC is at the crew and platoon levels. In preparing their units for the NTC, the training deficiency that leaders

> can't overcome very easily is a lack of skills or a lack of ability to execute down at the lowest level. We are constantly running into the situation where task forces develop good plans that they cannot execute, simply because the skills are not there at the lowest levels to make it happen. I'm not talking about exotic fancy plans, I'm talking about just nut[s] and bolts kind of attacking and defending.
>
> If they don't have leaders at the platoon level [E-5 through E-7] that know how to quickly and effectively assess the situation and to supervise and make every minute count ... it doesn't make any difference how well a task force commander laid out those goose eggs.
>
> They are not going to win when the OPFOR comes rolling at them with 160 vehicles. So I would urge units over and over again to work on building the primary building block, which is down at platoon level. If we get platoons that can execute, the other things fall into place pretty quickly.[12]

Figures 4.3 and 4.4 reflect observer/controller evaluations of small-unit training through evaluation of thirty-three platoons during a recent rotation at the NTC.[13]

The performance ratings for these platoons is consistent with the overall unit performance trend at the NTC over the past several years as reflected in Figure 4.2. Unfortunately, the great majority of platoons were rated "below standard" or "poor" with only 6.5 percent rated as exceeding standard. Confusion often arises at the NTC about standards of unit performance, with unit commanders often claiming exceedingly high levels of performance that are in sharp contrast with more objective

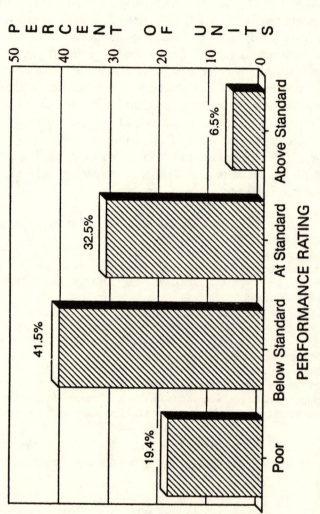

FIGURE 4.3 — Platoon Performance at NTC Rated By: Observer/Controllers (*Source:* NTC Focused Rotation 88-5)

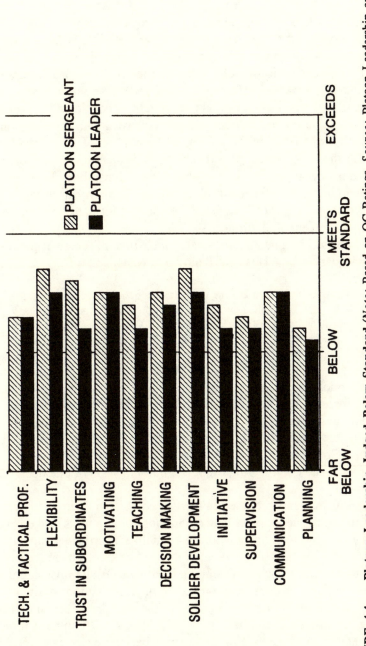

FIGURE 4.4 — Platoon Leadership Judged Below Standard (*Note*: Based on OC Ratings. *Source*: Platoon Leadership and Combat Performance Leadership and Management Technical Area, Army Research Institute, 1988.)

evaluations. This is reflected in the sharply different evaluations of performance for the same thirty-three platoons when the observer/controller and subject matter expert evaluations in the preceding figure are compared to company commander evaluations for the same thirty-three platoons shown in Figure 4.5.[14]

While self-evaluations such as those reflected in Figure 4.5 are no doubt sincere, they should not be considered as unbiased, objective evaluations. Such subjective evaluations should be considered in light of the overall tendency that officers have to overestimate their personal performance when compared to that of their peers. For example, as Figure 4.6 shows, between 60 percent and 70 percent of the lieutenants and captains in year groups 1980 through 1986 believe their performance places them in the top 10 percent of all officers in their year group, with over 90 percent of these officers believing their performance placed them in the top 20 percent of all officers.[15]

As expressed by one knowledgeable long-time observer of platoon-level performance at the NTC, the reality of it is that

> We in the Army have been kidding ourselves about how long it takes to get good at this stuff. . . . I thought I was a real hot-shot platoon leader. Now that I've watched over 300 battles out here [NTC] and seen what it really takes to win, I realize I didn't know anything. We've got to keep our leaders . . . with their men longer or we're going to lose our ass.[16]

This conclusion was reinforced by a U.S. commander of the opposing forces (OPFOR) at the NTC. He concluded that Soviet forces, who keep their soldiers in the same units for their entire service period, "have a better chance of winning a non nuclear battle in Europe." He stated that Soviet units "are better schooled in the fundamentals of massing force and coordinating firepower through years of practice in the field."[17]

The measurements reflected in the preceding figures in this chapter firmly support the conclusion that we are not training units at the NTC. Most officers involved agree with this conclusion privately, but often follow it with the statement that at least the leaders involved are receiving training that is almost as good as being in combat. While this statement might be true, data leader training received in prior rotations to the NTC is not being reflected in the performance of these leaders' current units at NTC. In one focused rotation, over 200 NCOs, 40 company grade officers, and approximately 400 service members were surveyed. Within this group average attendance at NTC, including the current rotation, was quite high as indicated for the following key positions: [18]

TABLE 4.1
Leader Attendance at the National Training Center

Position*	Times at NTC
Company CO	4 times
First Sergeant	3 times
Platoon Sergeant	3.5 times
Platoon Leader	2.5 times

Note: Prior attendance not necessarily in current position.

These data raise serious questions about the values of training leaders alone, without their units on a long-term basis. In this survey, soldiers had been in their units an average of only six months and 20 percent of them had been assigned as fillers just for the NTC. The correlations or relationship of unit performance with soldiers' and leaders' length of time in unit were quite high at .54 for crew or squad leader and .33 for soldiers.[19] These findings do not stand alone in their implications for effective unit training. Other reports have raised the issue earlier. One assessment of unit performance at the NTC found that platoon leader effectiveness was "marginally to slightly effective" or average based on subject matter experts and observer/controller ratings. Other reports offer similar conclusions.[20]

The discouraging conclusion is that the Army is not able to demonstrate any lasting benefit for unit performance by training at the NTC. At best, individual leaders might benefit but this experience does not appear to significantly affect unit performance at the NTC through any cumulative gain of leader experience. The desired overall unit training strategy of training prior to the NTC, evaluation at the NTC, and follow-up training based on NTC experience is not remotely possible for units given the current manpower and personnel systems, which create the turbulent environment within which Army training must currently exist.

The negative effects on unit training resulting from the invisible wall erected by the personnel system are manifested primarily in the unabated personnel turbulence (see Chapter 5), the low number of quality NCOs in combat units (see Chapter 6), and the deleterious effects of the Enlisted Personnel Management System (EPMS) (see Chapter 8). These effects stifle NCO motivation and initiative and prevent bonding necessary for effective leadership at the small combat unit level (see Chapter 7).

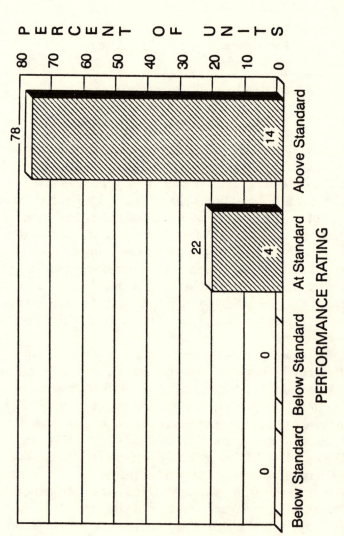

FIGURE 4.5 — Platoon Performance at NTC Rated By: Company Commander (*Source:* NTC Focused Rotation 88-5)

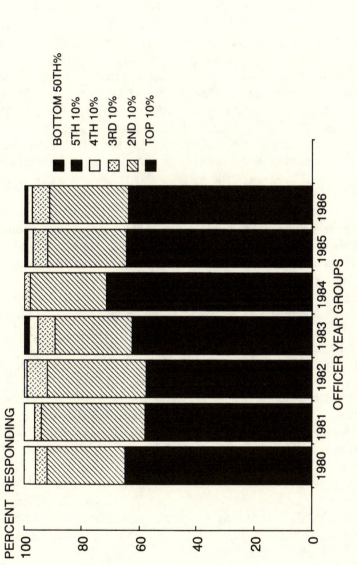

FIGURE 4.6 — **Perceived Performance in Comparison to Other Officers** (*Source:* Project Porteus. Personnel Utilization Technical Area, Army Research Institute, 1988.)

The normal process of unit and personnel system assignments creates such a volume of personnel changes within units that the reference to personnel turbulence is not unwarranted. Unfortunately, it has been part of the U.S. Army scene for so long it has become accepted as normal by many within the Army. To date the fact that the U.S. Army is the only major army in the world that tolerates such a system and its dysfunctional effects on combat effectiveness has been largely ignored by Army leaders. The inability of the COHORT program to deal effectively with turbulence and the increasing awareness of the harmful effects of turbulence on unit proficiency should challenge Army complacency. In 1985 LT. Gen. Walter F. Ulmer, then commanding general at Fort Hood, recognized that "Because of turbulence in the organization, you've got to keep teaching and coaching and reviewing SOP (Standard Operating Procedures), and drilling over and over again in today's Army. You have to fix things several times — they don't stay fixed. . . ."[21]

The greatest damage done by turbulence is at the crew, squad, and platoon levels. At these levels turbulence disrupts the enduring relationship between leaders and members of the unit necessary for leadership to develop based on mutual trust, professional values, and confidence in unit proficiency and effectiveness. Table 4.2 and Chapter 5 make clear that turbulence in the Army remains at extremely high levels and its effects continue to hinder unit training seriously.

The effect of such turbulence was made clear recently at the highest levels when the Chief of Staff reported after a 1988 visit to an armored division that "training preparation" for the NTC is the key to unit performance at the NTC and that the division, preparing to rotate to the NTC, reported that "the biggest distracter is the personnel turbulence. . . . There were only 14% of the M2/M3 [Bradley fighting vehicles] qualified crews available for the rotation [NTC] where 59 of 60 crews were qualified the previous October. . . . In addition . . . they had to rearrange every tank crew in the battalion."[22]

The gap between marginal levels of unit performance and the levels of excellence that a unit should achieve if it is a first-rate unit is in some part explained in the U.S. Army by the preceding discussion of continued turbulence and its potent effects, which neutralize much of the benefit potentially available from unit training.

Two additional factors also must be considered in explaining the gap between measured marginal unit performance and the levels of excellence necessary to win on the battlefield. These factors are the quality of small-unit leaders and the unintended but negative influences of moving away from the traditional function of the NCO Corps and patterning the

TABLE 4.2
Stability of Platoon Sergeants Is Related to Independent Assessments of Leadership and Combat Effectiveness at the NTC

THE LONGER A PLATOON SGT. WAS IN HIS UNIT, THE BETTER WAS THE RATED LEADERSHIP AND PERFORMANCE OF HIS UNIT.

	NTC MEASURE		
	PLT. LDR. LEADERSHIP	PLT. SGT. LEADERSHIP	PLT. EFFECTIVENESS
PLT. SGT. TIME IN UNIT	.53*	.58*	.43*

	NTC RATING**	
PLT. SGT. TIME IN UNIT	PSG LEADERSHIP	PLATOON EFFECTIVENESS
0-6 MOS.	2.7	3.0
7-12 MOS.	3.1	3.2
OVER 12 MOS.	4.0	3.8

*p < .05 N23 PLATOONS
**SCALE GOES FROM 1-5 WITH 3 = MARGINALLY EFFECTIVE

Source: NTC Focused Rotation on Leader Effectiveness, No. 86-13.

management of NCOs after the Officer Personnel Management System (OPMS) through an Enlisted Personnel Management System (EPMS). The "apeing" of OPMS by EPMS has had far-reaching but subtle and generally unrecognized negative effects on the NCO Corps. The recent tendency for NCOs to become careerists and move away from joining troops and units is more fully discussed in Chapter 8. The purpose here is to discuss the effects of EPMS and the related tendency of the most qualified NCOs to pursue careers away from long-term assignments with troop units and the resulting negative effects on training and unit performance.

These factors were recently hinted at in the August 1987 version of the Leader Development Study.[23] It quotes well-known leadership expert Lt. Gen. Walter F. Ulmer (ret.) as stating that "We are far from capitalizing on the human potential in our Army. . . . We are not as good as we can and must be. . . . Our major difficulties derive from . . . a lack of adequate conceptual basis for *selecting* and developing leaders and for creating and sustaining a proper climate within our commands."[24]

The issue of selecting the best-qualified small-unit leaders is directly related to effective unit training and ultimately with unit performance in combat. Substantial evidence exists that relates leader quality to unit performance in training and in combat. The most recent and convincing discussions focus on the combat performance of the Israeli defense forces and their systems for selecting small-unit leaders.[25]

The case for selecting the best-qualified unit leaders is compelling. The case is similar for all of the combat arms but for consistency, examples are drawn primarily from the U.S. Army armor force. The case is made compelling by starting with the fact that only 4 percent of the Army's strength (armor personnel) contribute about 38 percent of the Army's conventional firepower.[26] Foremost is the recognition that while the armor force is equipment oriented and relies extensively on technology, the final and decisive element in battle is the human element. Victory in the end is dependent on initiative, especially at the junior leader level, and it requires the "mental alertness, aggressiveness and ability to think, act, and quickly seize the initiative in highly mobile platforms possessing remarkable firepower."[27] To meet these criteria for performance in combat, quality must be defined in terms of actual performance in combat tasks along with the practical need at least to match the quality in leaders and soldiers available to the top-performing armies of the world. This, for example, must be a basic consideration when analyzing the competing strategies of the United States and the

Soviet Union, or any other potential adversary. We know the Soviet Army utilizes a sophisticated selection, classification, and assignment system and that they have access to large numbers of quality personnel (the top third of the Soviet population), many of whom are no doubt placed in small-unit leadership positions in the Soviet Army.

The major factor in Israeli victories over the years in the Middle East has been the quality of IDF small-unit leaders and the selection of these combat leaders (officers and NCOs) from among those who scored in the top one-third in KABA scores (similar to U.S. Armed Forces Qualification Test [AFQT]).[28] Therefore *quality* is defined here as being in the top one-third in mental ability as well as performing well on motivational, psychomotor, and spatial tests from the Army's Project A. Such a definition would allow the U.S. Army at least to match the human potential available to other armies. This definition of quality could be expanded to include all the upper 50 percent measured by mental category. However, this would mean accepting significant degradations in combat performance that are currently not accepted by other top-performing armies in the world.[29] Further, as Chapter 6 makes clear, the U.S. Army currently has available to it much of the necessary quality to meet its leadership needs. However, to utilize this asset correctly will require recognition of the need for necessary policy changes.

Critical to achieving this vision is selection of top-quality NCOs as junior leaders beginning with those selected as tank commanders and squad leaders in the infantry and other branches. It is not necessary to repeat here the data and conclusions relating soldier quality to performance discussed previously. Table 4.3 makes clear the essential need to have the best-qualified leaders in small units as well as quality soldiers. Based on an established relationship of soldier trainability with soldier quality measured by the AFQT,[30] the table demonstrates the expected increase in crew/unit performance as the trainability (quality) of the unit leader is also increased.[31]

In many respects the NCO Corps is in overall better shape than ever before. As a result of a sophisticated development system NCOs are better educated and more highly motivated, displaying in large part pride and confidence in their duties. Yet these NCO qualities are not being utilized fully in the training of our units and as a result, demonstrated unit performance remains well below the levels of excellence necessary to win on today's battlefields.

A third major factor affecting unit training and performance is unrecognized but evident malaise in the EPMS, and manifest in the "confusion about the role of the NCO and his duties."[32] It is also evident

TABLE 4.3
Percent Increase in Crew Performance

GUNNER MENTAL CATEGORY	$\dfrac{M60}{M1}$ TC MENTAL CATEGORY				
	I	II	IIIA	IIIB	IV
I	$\dfrac{55.0}{44.2}$				
II		$\dfrac{46.4}{37.7}$			
IIIA			$\dfrac{38.8}{31.6}$		
IIIB				$\dfrac{21.3}{17.5}$	
IV					BASE CASE

Source: Paper by F. J. Brown on combat leaders for the Armor Force, 1985.

in the discussions about the primary function of the NCO Corps and the authority and responsibilities necessary for sergeants to discharge their function. The migration of NCOs away from their traditional role of linking soldiers to unit and the much-cited lack of NCO initiative in units appears to be related to trainability issues and reflected in the leader quality data shown in Table 4.4. It must be emphasized that this is not a minority issue. The migration of top NCOs has occurred across the board among black and Hispanic as well as white NCOs. The fault rests not with NCOs but with the structure of the system (EPMS) and the resulting ambiguity about the primary functions of the NCO Corps and the need to reassert that the NCO's primary job is small-unit leader with the tasks of training his unit and leading it in combat.

If the U.S. Army is to compete on an equal force-to-force basis with other world-class armies, it must draw its small-unit leaders (e.g., tank commanders, gunners, and squad leaders) from among the most qualified soldiers available. In practical terms this means from at least among the top one-third in mental quality. Table 4.4, for example, displays the huge deficiency faced by the U.S. armor force in 1988. As noted in an earlier chapter, the percentages are almost identical for MOS-19E (M-60 tank) and reflect an enduring pattern within the armor corps.

The numbers and percentages are alarming. They show that the U.S. armor force has only 396 quality NCOs out of 1,495 (26 percent) in the proper grade (E-6) to act as tank commanders for the Army's newest and most potent conventional weapons system. To insist that the majority of sergeants E-6, in MOS 19K, who are in the bottom half in quality, can perform optimally as tank commanders is to deny all of the preceding performance data, and the historical evidence associated with quality leadership and battlefield outcomes as well as the fact that much evidence points to Soviet classification and selection procedures that place the most qualified of Soviet youth in similar positions in the Soviet Army. Finally, the U.S. Army cannot in good conscience place young American soldiers under tank commanders and other small-unit leaders who do not possess all of the necessary qualities to ensure the best possible chance of success and survival in battle.

Even if the 611 top one-third quality sergeants E-5 were taken away from other duties such as gunner and combined with the 395 sergeant E-6 M-1 tank commanders, the total would be far short of the number necessary to provide top-quality commanders for the M-1 tank force. Unfortunately even this meager provision of top-quality NCOs for the armor force has been significantly eroded by assignment away from combat armor units. Supposedly higher-priority assignments such as the Army recruiting command and drill instructor as well as other special duty assignments bleed off the quality NCOs, leaving few for duty with the troops. Spot checks among several divisions show that few top-third quality NCOs find their way to duty with troop units. While acknowledging that many quality NCOs go to special assignments such as basic training, recruiting, and other assignments, the centralized Military Personnel Command (formerly MILPERCEN) is unable to ensure that top-quality NCOs assigned to the field are assigned positions with combat units. All too often these NCOs are assigned to the peacetime Army with primarily administrative noncombat duties.

Given these considerations and, as noted previously, upon the basis of spot checks throughout the Army, it is estimated that of the already meager sum of 396 top-quality E-6 M-1 tank commanders available to the U.S. Army, less than 200 are probably assigned to M-1 tank units at any one time. If General (ret.) William E. DePuy is correct in stating that

TABLE 4.4
Armor NCO Quality for MOS-19K (M1-Tank)
(as of November 1, 1987)

MENTAL CATEGORY (TOP THIRD)	E-5	E-6	E-7
I	59 (2.47%)	58 (3.88%)	37 (3.97%)
II	552 (23.09%)	338 (22.61%)	257 (27.58%)
	GRADE		

% REFLECTS PERCENTAGE OF GRADE IN MENTAL CATEGORY

Source: Defense Manpower Data Center.

overall M-1 tank performance can be measured by the formula $Ps = Ph \times Pe$ (where Ps = system performance, Ph = human performance, and Pe = equipment performance),[33] then the U.S. Army is falling far short of realizing the overall potential in the M-1 tank system. This is no doubt reflected in the fact that greater than 50 percent of the M-1s fail to open fire on the battlefield at the NTC; this is most often attributed to lack of leader initiative.

The situation is not easily corrected in the event of war. There is no easy fix such as hurriedly reassigning quality NCOs from noncombat assignments to combat positions in the event of war. It is unlikely these personnel shifts could be efficiently made in time and even if some were, we know from prior combat experience and the NTC that even the highest-quality leaders need sufficient time (months) with a unit in order to make it into a high-performing unit. This time, in all likelihood, will not be available. To quote from a recent Soviet military commander interviewed on ABC news under the ground rules of glasnost, "The side who fires the first shot and starts the war in Europe will win."[34] This agrees with our knowledge of Soviet strategy, the role of surprise, and the Soviet need to win a war in Europe quickly before the United States can fully mobilize. In any such scenario the U.S. armor force in all likelihood will fight the war with about 200 top-quality tank commanders in place and not all of them in Europe. In addition, most of these tank commanders will have been with their current crews only six to nine weeks.

Through EPMS the Army has been making attempts to improve the situation. To date, however, the attempts have been ineffectual. The nature of the effort has been to fine tune and tweak EPMS in order to ratchet up NCO quality in the combat arms. As stated earlier, there is a curious reluctance for Army leaders at the top- and midrange levels to follow back to their roots within the personnel system the causes (turbulence, quality, EPMS, etc.) of marginal unit performance.

Table 4.5, when compared to the numbers in Table 4.4, makes clear the ineffectual nature of the Army's multiyear attempt to improve the quality of small-unit combat leadership.

After two years of effort, the personnel managers have had minimal success in ratcheting up the quality of NCOs in the combat arms. In the critical MOS of 19K, for NCO leaders for the M-1 tank, we have only been able to increase the number of quality E-5 gunners by 226 for a total of 611. In the critical position of M-1 tank commander of staff sergeant (E-6) we gained only 195 for a total of 396 quality tank commanders. Although these numbers change quickly, the critical fact is that over the

TABLE 4.5
Armor NCO Quality for MOS-19K (M1-Tank)
(as of November 1, 1985)

		E-5	E-6	E-7
MENTAL CATEGORY	I	63 (3.63%)	46 (5.14%)	38 (5.87%)
	II	322 (18.56%)	155 (17.32%)	153 (23.65%)
	IIIA	213 (12.28%)	116 (12.96%)	113 (17.47%)
	IIIB	506 (29.16%)	286 (31.96%)	222 (34.31%)
	IV	631 (36.37%)	292 (32.63%)	121 (18.70%)

GRADE

% REFLECTS PERCENTAGE OF GRADE
IN MENTAL CATEGORY

Source: Defense Manpower Data Center.

long term only about 25 percent of key combat leadership is in the top one-third and that of these, only about half are actually serving with troops as combat leaders. The inability to provide top-quality crews for the thousands of tanks in the Army's combat units seriously degrades the overall system performance and significantly limits the combat potential and warfighting capabilities of American ground forces.

These limitations apply across the board to all of the U.S. Army combat arms. For example, in the critical MOS of 11M, which provides leadership for the Army's M-2 Bradley fighting vehicle, there are only 194 top-quality sergeants (E-6) out of about 900 available to lead this complex system comprised of soldiers and high technology. This is only an increase of 97 quality NCOs in the last two years. The picture is just as serious in the Army's basic infantry MOS 11B. At the end of 1985, the Army had 1,508 top-quality E-6 (MOS 11B) infantry NCOs. Three years later, in 1988, that number was 1,814 out of 6,669, which still falls far short of the thousands required if the Army is to provide the leadership necessary to produce high-performing units capable of matching the human capability of other armies.[35]

Even if the definition of quality leaders was expanded to include all NCOs within the top one-half of AFQT scores, the improvements in numbers would be minimal. For example, if mental category IIIA NCOs were included, this would add only 177 staff sergeants to MOS 11M for the M-2 Bradley fighting vehicle, and 331 tank commanders (E-6) to the M-1 Abrams tank.[36] These are insignificant increases in total end-strength numbers, yet even to achieve these marginal increases, significant degradation in performance must be accepted.

"Quality up front" should become the policy slogan for the NCO Corps. In the three major combat branches, infantry, armor, and artillery, the combined number of quality NCOs the Army can expect currently to have available at any one time to fight the "decisive" war is approximately 7,032 E-5s, 4,195 E-6s, and 2,679 E-7s.[37] Compared to this meager number of top-quality combat arms NCOs, of whom approximately one-half are assigned to combat units, the Army currently has within its overall ranks 82,511 top-quality NCOs: 37,861 E-5s, 26,601 E-6s, and 18,049 E-7s.[38] This number equitably represents minorities and is numerous enough to satisfy the need for quality small combat unit leadership. The Army must put some of this quality forward into its combat units. As currently assigned, many of these quality NCOs man an inefficiently structured staff function that causes the Army to pay a large price for a relatively small return in warfighting capability.

The negative effects of turbulence and inadequate small-unit leadership on unit performance are relatively straightforward. EPMS, however, has second- and third-order effects on training and unit performance that are more subtle and difficult to relate. Nevertheless the assumptions and organizational policies that underlie and govern the Army's Enlisted Personnel Management System appear to have deleterious effects on NCO motivation, initiative, and career planning. These policies significantly distract NCOs from their traditional functions of training and leading troops in combat.

NOTES

1. General Wickham, chief of staff, U.S. Army. Address to Deputy Chief of Staff for Personnel, General Officer Proponents Conference, Twin Bridges Marriott, Washington, D.C., March 11, 1987.

2. The NTC is located at Fort Irwin, California. It encompasses 640,000 acres and provides a fourteen-day combined arms force-on-force, live-fire field training exercise. It trains mechanized battalion/task forces in the Continental U.S. (CONUS) to fight and win the air/land battle in a mid- to high-intensity environment. There are currently fourteen annual rotations that train two task forces per rotation. Beginning in FY 1988, the brigade commander and his staff were evaluated. In 1990 the NTC will expand to evaluate the heavy brigade consisting of three battalion task forces and associated combat support and combat service support elements. The Joint Readiness Training Center (JRTC) is another of the CTCs.

3. General Accounting Office report to the Secretary of the Army, "Army National Training Center's Potential Has Not Been Realized" (Washington, D.C.: General Accounting Office, July 1986).

4. Army Chief of Staff Memorandum, "Visit to Fort Irwin," May 3, 1988.

5. George C. Wilson, "In Mock Combat, 'Soviets' Win Again and Again," *Washington Post*, February 22, 1982, A8.

6. John A. Spears, Memo for Record, Subject: NTC Trend Line Analysis, Training and Doctrine Command (TRADOC), February 11, 1988.

7. Ibid.

8. Ibid.

9. See U.S. Army Armor School briefing chart "Observation" on unit problems at the NTC in 1988 — "Junior Leaders' Lack of Initiative" and Sam Endicott and Earl Pence, "NTC Leadership Lessons Learned," (unpublished report, TRADOC, 1987).

10. These dollar costs are conservative estimates and do not include dollars spent by many other organizations and agencies in support of the NTC. Nor do they include the operational and transportation costs for FY 1988 and FY 1989.

11. Larry E. Word, "Observations From Three Years at the National Training Center" (Army Research Institute Field Unit at Presidio of Monterey, Calif., January 1987).

12. Ibid., 7–8.

13. Robert Holz, "ARI Leadership Technical Area Report on NTC Rotation 88-5," (Alexandria, Va.: ARI, 1988).

14. Ibid.

15. Glenda Nogami, Department of the Army, Project Proteus Briefing, 1988.

16. George C. Wilson, "In Mock Combat," p. A8.

17. Ibid.

18. Holz, "Report."

19. Ibid.

20. See, for example, D. L. Rachford and P. T. Twohig, "ARI Working Paper 88-06, Platoon Leader Platoon Sergeant Focused Rotation at the NTC," December 1986; and Endicott and Pence, NTC Leadership Lessons Learned.

21. Deborah G. Meyer, "More Authority Responsibility Placed on NCOs' Shoulder at Fort Hood," *Armed Forces Journal*, May 1985, 74.

22. Chief of staff visit memorandum, May 23, 1988, p. 6.

23. Major General Sullivan, *Leader Development Study*, 1987 ed. (U.S. Army Combined Arms Center, Fort Leavenworth, Kans.) 3.

24. Ibid.

25. See Chapter 6 for a more complete discussion.

26. Frederic J. Brown, Preface to unpublished paper on "Combat Readiness for the Armor Force" (U.S. Armor Center, Fort Knox, Ky., July 1985), 1.

27. Brown, Preface.

28. The basis for Israeli selection of small-unit leaders (NCOs) is based on measurements of performance related to quality very similar to U.S. Army performance measures in Project A described in notes for Chapter 3.

29. An examination of the figures in Chapter 3 that relate performance and mental quality reflect significant differences in levels of expected combat performance between top, middle, and bottom thirds.

30. Joyce Shields, "The Army's Quality Need," in Robert Philips et al., unpublished paper on "Combat Readiness for the Armor Force" (U.S. Armor Center, Fort Knox, Ky., 1985), 2–9.

31. Robert Philips et al., unpublished paper on "Combat Readiness for the Armor Force." (U.S. Armor Center, Fort Knox, Ky., 1985), 2–13.

32. Sullivan, *Leader Development Study*, 22.

33. William E. DePuy, "Technology and Manpower: Army Perspective" in *The All-Volunteer Force After a Decade* (Washington, D.C.: Pergamon-Brassey's, 1983), 131.

34. ABC "Evening News," May 23, 1988.

35. Army Personnel Master File and Defense Manpower Data Center, 1988.

36. Based on spot checks with the Army Personnel Command, Alexandria, Va., and Army units and posts..

37. Army Personnel Master File and Defense Manpower Data Center.

38. Ibid.

5

PERSONNEL TURBULENCE

The bedrock foundation upon which cohesive units must be built is unit integrity and stability. The human potential of an Army can only be maximized through units that bind the soldier, through his leaders, to dominant group norms that result in individual commitment, values, and behavior that promote unit and Army goals. To achieve this the unit must become the dominant force in controlling the individual soldier and his day-to-day behavior. Small-unit leadership is the essential factor in developing such behavior in stable units. Unit leadership must be based on personal relationships between soldiers and leaders that emphasize professional values and personal trust and place unit rules and goals above individual goals. This is currently not the situation. The process through which the Army personnel structure functions is an individual-oriented process and turbulence is one result of putting individual over unit priorities. The current status of personnel turbulence and its effects on the Army are outlined below and further supported in this chapter.

- Unit integrity and stability is requisite for high-performing, combat-ready units capable of winning over other armies.
- Measures of personnel turbulence at the vital small-unit level persist at about 150 percent annually.
- In spite of the COHORT program, turbulence remains "uncontrolled, unmeasured, unreported and seemingly unacknowledged."
- Effects are significant; for example, the U.S. Army provides more live training rounds (e.g., tank) than does the Soviet Army but stabilized Soviet tank crews fire approximately 200 percent more training rounds per crew than do U.S. crews.

- Personnel turbulence in the U.S. Army continues unabated and is preventing the achievement of highly trained, high-performing units.

Personnel turbulence does its greatest damage when it is widespread at small-unit levels and disrupts the relationships between team, squad, and platoon leaders and soldiers. It is at the squad, platoon, and company levels that the primary phenomena of leadership take place because it is here that the individual soldier is convinced to take actions, such as advancing under fire, that threaten his individual well-being. The small-unit leader must link the goals and missions of the Army to the needs and goals of soldiers in crews, squads, and platoons. To do this successfully, the small-unit leader creates group rules that deemphasize soldier individualism and promote group norms that put the unit first. In cohesive units, group norms put the unit first. The soldier is constantly reminded of the expectations of his buddies and his leaders. In this way, the individual soldier's sense of responsibility to his squad, platoon, and ultimately the Army is reflected by his taking the professional values of his sergeants and company officers as the primary determinant of his day-to-day behavior.

To date the U.S. Army has not managed to produce units characterized by the personnel stability and unit integrity necessary to allow unit leaders the opportunity to build cohesive units, either COHORT or non-COHORT.

In addition to its major effect as a promoter of cohesive units, unit stability is also significantly linked to unit performance. Recent assessments at the National Training Center (NTC) related turbulence of small-unit leaders to poor platoon performance. In relating the leadership of twenty-three platoon sergeants (correlation of .58) to platoon effectiveness (correlation of .43) those platoon sergeants who had been in their unit less than six months were generally rated as ineffective with a rating of 2.7 (5-point scale with 3 = marginally effective) and their platoons rated at 3.0 or marginally effective. Contrasted with this, platoon sergeants assigned over twelve months had much higher leadership ratings of 4.0 and platoon effectiveness ratings of 3.8.[1] Table 5.1 presents further correlations of personnel turbulence with improved unit performance. Over 530 soldiers including 198 NCOs in thirty-one different platoons were surveyed. Of particular note is the correlation of .54 for performance for squad/crew leaders. These leaders had over six months with their squads with at least 75 percent of their squad or crew remaining stable during this period.[2] It is interesting to speculate what gains in performance could be expected if we were able to relate performance to measures of stability of eighteen or twenty-four months as do many top armies.

In a prior examination of the effects of personnel turbulence and length of unit training time, researchers Kent Eaton and G. Neff demonstrated in an examination of 255 tank crews in five U.S. armor battalions in Europe that tank commander and gunner turbulence can be an important factor in tank crew performance. The more time a tank commander and gunner trained together the more rapidly fire was brought to bear on the target.[3] These measurements support conclusions that the improvements in crew coordination and teamwork that come with unit stability are reflected in unit performance.

In an interesting effort to assess the effects of personnel turmoil defined as those changes that take place only within the small unit, one researcher measured squad performance in live-fire exercises against various personnel changes within the squad to include changes of both soldiers and squad leader. The conclusion was that more changes were an accurate predictor of lower scores in squad live-fire exercises. Most significantly, those squads with long-term leadership were usually higher performers than squads with new leaders, especially in exercises with higher stress.[4]

The degree of turbulence in the U.S. Army and its pernicious effects have been long suspected. With much publicity and flogging of the personnel system in the late 1970s and early 1980s, firm and "locked-in" policies were implemented finally to deal with the problem of turbulence.

TABLE 5.1
Correlations of Platoon Turbulence with NTC Performance

LENGTH OF TIME WITH SQUAD	
SQUAD/CREW MEMBER	.33
SQUAD/CREW LEADER	.54
MONTHS IN COMPANY	
SQUAD/CREW MEMBER	.33
SQUAD/CREW LEADER	.32

Source: Robert Holz, NTC Focused Rotation 88-5.

General Edward C. Meyer, at the time chief of staff of the Army, demonstrated that he understood the connection between the individual-oriented personnel system, turbulence, and unit performance in 1983 when he wrote the following:

> I'd complained a lot about personnel in the past. I was also aware of a lot of spears stuck in its carcass over the years. The history of failed ventures to resuscitate the individual replacement system was impressive. Still the net result added up to excessive and debilitating soldier turbulence which precluded our units . . . from achieving desired readiness standards.[5]

On this basis, the most recent assault on the individual replacement system and personnel turbulence began. Extensive studies identified the causes and degree of turbulence. The COHORT program was the major effort initiated finally to bring personnel turbulence under control and create cohesive units.

Almost ten years have passed, and great effort has been devoted toward the implementation of these policies. COHORT has been adjusted and fine tuned, unfortunately with little effect. To the question of whether COHORT has decreased personnel turbulence and led to the creation of cohesive units, the short answer is — No. Turbulence in both COHORT and non-COHORT units remains at approximately the same high levels as previously measured. To quote from a recent and definitive paper on the state of turbulence in the U.S. Army, turbulence remains "relatively uncontrolled, unmeasured, unreported and seemingly unacknowledged."[6] Further, cohesion is evident in few COHORT units. Some nascent increase in cohesion was brought about through COHORT, but only in a few COHORT units (approximately 20 percent) where turbulence was temporarily lulled and adequate small-unit leadership was available to develop some measure of cohesion.[7]

However, for the great majority of units in the Army the situation remains unchanged. This includes COHORT as well as non-COHORT units. Some recent measures of turbulence are disingenuous and are little better than apologias for a policy that is not working. For example, one report states that turbulence for Forces Command (FORSCOM) was 23 percent (less than 20 percent for E-1 through E-4) for approximately an eleven-month period; the report goes on to imply that all is well by declaring that "the replacement vs attrition rates are nicely balanced at this level."[8] Such a report would indeed be encouraging if it were a valid measure of turbulence.

Turbulence cannot be measured validly from the Department of the Army level by looking at only external sources of turbulence at the battalion level. Such measurements miss the point. If cohesion is created by long-term association between soldiers and their immediate leaders, then measures of turbulence must take place at these levels. Such measurements reflect the time soldiers have been together with their tank commander or squad leader and reflect the time available for trust to develop, for skills to be demonstrated, and for teamwork to evolve. If the ultimate purpose of COHORT is to promote cohesive units and thereby maximize unit performance through gaining the most out of training, teamwork, and the professional influence of small-unit leaders, then the most meaningful measure of personnel turbulence is the time that the soldier spends with his immediate small-unit leaders at the crew, team, squad, and platoon levels.

As Lawrence R. Boice and T. Owen Jacobs note:

> To the Personal Agency assignment officer, movement has not occurred unless a geographic relocation results in a Permanent Change of Station (PCS). To the battalion commander, movement occurs when a soldier leaves his battalion. But to the squad leader, it makes little difference whether a soldier departing his squad remains in that battalion or has PCS orders to Tanzania. The impact is the same, a new arrival must be assimilated into that primary combat group to take the place of the departing squad member. The "team" becomes a new team as a result of new membership. . . . The impact of high turbulence is that soldiers get tired of making unprofitable investments of time and energy to build new teams, and gradually cease to do that work. The end state is a relative lack of caring, and a low level of both horizontal and vertical bonding.[9]

Figure 5.1 shows a more current and valid comparison of personnel turbulence for E-1 through E-4 soldiers in combat units in the United States and U.S. Army Europe (USAREUR). The figure compares COHORT units with all combat units in Europe and the United States and indicates that COHORT makes little difference to personnel turbulence.[10]

Figure 5.2 makes clear that actual turbulence in units is much greater than reported. Only half (approximately) of all battalion losses are generated by the Department of the Army. Within battalions turbulence is much greater with many more soldiers changing jobs for each loss to the battalion. Changes between soldiers and leaders is even greater. Prior review conservatively indicates that a reported rate of 24 percent is an actual rate of about 64 percent personnel turbulence at company level.[11] It is clear that most turbulence is officially ignored and unreported. The Unit Status Report (USR) does not include internal turbulence within the battalion. In fact, Army Regulation 220–1 specifically excludes the reporting by battalions of internal sources of turbulence.[12]

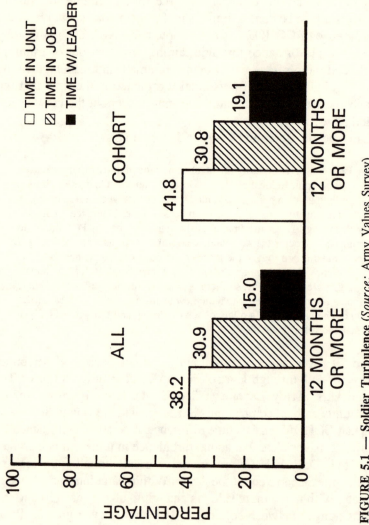

FIGURE 5.1 — Soldier Turbulence (*Source*: Army Values Survey)

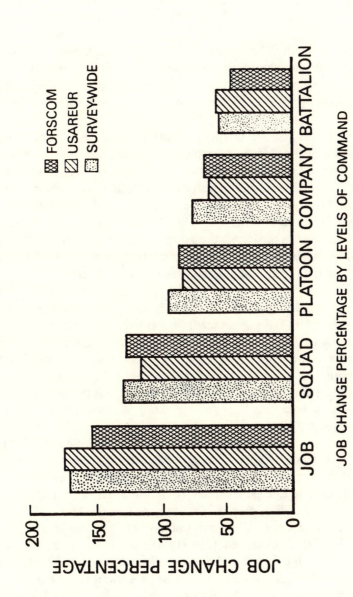

FIGURE 5.2 — Annual Job Change by Soldiers at Different Unit Levels (*Source:* ARI Briefing)

83

Turbulence among small-unit COHORT leaders is as great as for grades E-1 through E-4. Recent turnover of key officers and noncommissioned officers at COHORT company, platoon, and squad levels is very high.[13]

As reported by their first-term soldiers (E-1 through E-4): 33 percent had two or more company commanders in one year; 47 percent had two or more platoon leaders in one year; 66 percent had two or more platoon sergeants in one year; and 65 percent had two or more squad leaders in one year.

Without controlling for quality of leadership, which is an extremely important variable, the effects of turbulence among specific key leaders at the small-unit level is seen in Figure 5.3.[14] The top scale shows that platoon leaders and sergeants as well as squad leaders view their units as more combat ready the longer they remain in the unit. The lower scale shows that soldiers (E-1 through E-4) believe their immediate leaders are more effective leaders the longer the leaders remain in the unit.

Personnel turbulence persists. Illustrative samples confirm the validity of the data. A recent assessment of tank crew turbulence in U.S. tank battalions in Europe shows a persistently high turnover rate among tank commanders and gunners. As we have seen previously, the stability of tank commanders and gunner teams is a key determinate of the ability of a tank crew to bring fire to bear on a target. This does not bode well for any future combat in Europe in view of a report which found that "In tank battalions of approximately 50 crews each, the master gunners recently indicated that over the preceding four-month period, only from four to twelve tank commander and gunner crew teams out of fifty, had remained together."[15]

In addition to the concern this finding and others like it should cause among Army leaders, second and third order effects are also felt throughout the system. An example of this became apparent to me at a recent conference in Europe that featured the commander in chief (CINC) of the U.S. Army in Europe as a luncheon speaker on Army training in Europe.[16] In comparing U.S. Army Europe training with Warsaw Pact training, the CINC observed that significant U.S. advantage was achieved through the fact that U.S. tanks in Europe fired 100 main gun training rounds per year while Soviet crews in Eastern Europe only fired 70 rounds per year. The implication was obvious that 30 extra training rounds per year contributed greatly toward making U.S. crews better trained should war come in Europe. After his luncheon comments the CINC privately acknowledged that crew turbulence was a significant problem for training effectiveness. However, it's not sure that he realized

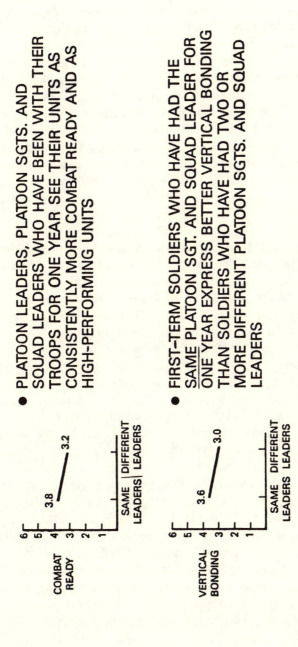

- PLATOON LEADERS, PLATOON SGTS. AND SQUAD LEADERS WHO HAVE BEEN WITH THEIR TROOPS FOR ONE YEAR SEE THEIR UNITS AS CONSISTENTLY MORE COMBAT READY AND AS HIGH-PERFORMING UNITS

- FIRST-TERM SOLDIERS WHO HAVE HAD THE SAME PLATOON SGT. AND SQUAD LEADER FOR ONE YEAR EXPRESS BETTER VERTICAL BONDING THAN SOLDIERS WHO HAVE HAD TWO OR MORE DIFFERENT PLATOON SGTS. AND SQUAD LEADERS

COMBAT READY

6
5
4   3.8
3   3.2
2
1

SAME | DIFFERENT
LEADERS | LEADERS

VERTICAL BONDING

6
5
4   3.6
3   3.0
2
1

SAME   DIFFERENT
LEADERS LEADERS

FIGURE 5.3 — Stability of Key NCOs and Officers Is Associated with Perceived Unit Effectiveness and Cohesion (*Source:* NTC Focused Rotation on Leader Effectiveness, No. 86-13.)

85

that the problem was as stark as the average U.S. tank commander gunner team only getting to fire approximately 33 rounds or less as a team while Soviet crews got to fire approximately 105 rounds or about 200 percent more rounds than U.S. crews during their one and a half years together as a team.

Consistent with the data on tank crews is another recent and independent analysis of personnel turbulence in a mechanized infantry battalion equipped with Bradley fighting vehicles (BFV). It was a very detailed look at *all* turbulence within the battalion over an eleven-month period.[17] The 472 Bradley fighting positions in the battalion were monitored for both external (in or out of battalion) and internal changes among units within the battalion.[18] The measurements were taken during the period following the introduction of the BFV into the battalion and new equipment training (NET). During this period, priority was placed on reducing personnel turbulence. As Table 5.2 shows, even with this added emphasis, full (nine-man) BFV squads were available for training with squad leaders (E-6) only 16 percent of the time or only four weeks together.[19] This is extremely important for training with the Bradley. The presence of sergeants with the requisite training and experience is essential for the conduct of training in the highly technological BFV. As Table 5.2 indicates, turbulence in these BFV units was significant in spite of the effort to stabilize units during NET training.

It should be noted that the measures in Table 5.2 are conservative. Probably a more realistic median time together for squad leader-gunner is six weeks rather than nine.[20] Either amount of time is grossly inadequate to provide the basis for the strong vertical bonding necessary to achieve the full potential of an infantry squad equipped with perhaps the most technologically advanced armored personnel carrier in the world with an infantry mission greatly increased in complexity over that of former "straight leg" infantry squads.

The dysfunctions attributed to personnel turbulence have been shown. The causes of turbulence are apparent. The most often-stated cause is the need to fill vacancies in units. In U.S. infantry, armor, and artillery units worldwide, turbulence in over 50 percent of a battalion's strength in a one-year period is caused by PCS orders or orders of other major headquarters above battalion level.[21] A turnover rate of over 50 percent a year would be intolerable for any commander intent upon building cohesion and unit performance. Worse still, however, is that in addition to the 50 percent turnover rate initiated by headquarters above battalion, there is much more serious turbulence within the battalion. Soldiers within battalions have an average of three different jobs per year

TABLE 5.2
Personnel Turbulence in a Mechanized Infantry Battalion

SQUAD INTEGRITY

COMBINATION	MEDIAN TIME TOGETHER IN WEEKS
SQUAD LEADER-GUNNER	9
SQUAD LEADER-GUNNER-ASSISTANT SQUAD LEADER	7
ENTIRE 9-MAN SQUAD	4

Source: Bradley Fighting Vehicle Training Effectiveness Analysis (TEA).

or about a 150 percent turbulence rate.[22] The most recent data available, cited earlier, indicate this approximate situation holds year after year.

On top of the personnel moves caused by PCS and other similar orders, the need by commanders to fill jobs at three times the rate of interbattalion changes causes such a degree of turbulence that the limits of the system to create cohesive and high-performing units are soon reached.[23] Much criticism is directed toward unit commanders for their high rates of internal turbulence. This criticism is not well directed. Instead it must be recognized that the overall system (i.e., Army organization) forces the unit commander to suboptimize. The system forces the commander to choose between maintaining personnel stability and maintaining operational readiness. The absolute requirement to keep tanks, artillery, and Bradley fighting vehicles operational, as well as meet countless other operational requirements, forces commanders to adopt policies such as cross-leveling to reassign and cross-train soldiers in order to meet operational and support requirements.[24] When such moves involve promotions or prospects for promotion the soldier himself is an eager participant in the turbulence. While many commanders acknowledge the benefits of cohesion, there is not universal agreement about the desirability of reduced turbulence and there does not appear to be a strong concern for cohesion when contrasted to the operational needs to keep tanks, artillery, and other equipment fully manned.

The "package" replacements system as currently structured and implemented will fall far short of the goal of producing stable cohesive units. While transporting groups of soldiers as packages during wartime will probably relieve some individual stress during wartime replacement, we should not expect such packages to do much toward producing cohesive fighting units. As structured these packages do not include small-unit leaders nor are they intended to be employed as integral small fighting units. Experience to date has shown these groups are being split up upon reaching their destinations and are being used as individual replacements or at best, they are being assigned in some cases as two-man teams. Indeed a recent survey of unit commanders and adjutants showed most intended to use such personnel packages as a source of individual replacements.[25] Again the requirements for operational readiness, the need to cross-level, fill vacancies, and cross-train have brought us to the limits of the system. Personnel turbulence continues unabated and is preventing the achievement of highly trained, high-performing cohesive units.

The direct causes of personnel turbulence in the Army have been widely studied and are generally recognized. But it is not sufficient to state that the individual replacement system is at fault. The causes are much deeper. They extend from fundamental system assumptions about career and personnel management as well as requirements for operational readiness. Perhaps most of all, the root cause is a failure of vision that has permitted personnel and training systems to evolve within which organizational structures and responsibilities are not well matched with functions. This fragmented, inefficient, structural-functional system has emerged on an ad hoc basis generally guided by a tendency to centralize functions at the Department of the Army level over the past fifteen years and has fallen short in its ability to produce first-rate combat units. It is also very likely that the limit of this system's ability to produce first-rate combat units has been reached significantly short of the standards necessary to win in war.

The needs is clear. The U.S. Army needs a personnel and training system that will allow unit commanders to achieve full operational readiness as well as build cohesive high-performing units. To achieve this a basic rule of systems theory must be recognized and accommodated. The rule simply stated is that a change made in one place in the system will eventually have an effect in many ways elsewhere in the system. In the present case such changes force the commander to suboptimize because the system prevents him from achieving operational readiness and building cohesive units at the same time. If the U.S. Army is ever to become a great army, it needs a system that allows commanders to achieve both.

NOTES

1. Robert Holz, "ARI Briefing on NTC Focused Rotation, 86-13."
2. Robert Holz, "ARI Briefing on NTC Focused Rotation, 88-5."
3. Kent Eaton and G. Neff, "ARI Tech Report 350," 28–29. The absence of positive data in targets hit is probably related to the inadequacy of using tank table VIII as a measure of performance. Table XII would possibly be a better test of crew ability to hit the target under combat conditions.
4. Mike McGee, "Forging Teamwork: Personnel Stabilization in Rifle Squads," Fort Leavenworth, Kans. Exec Net Paper 1-87.
5. General E. C. Meyer, *White Paper,* 1980, 8. Cited in Thomas E. Kelly, "Towards Excellence: The Army Develops a New Personnel System," 14. Submitted to the Alfred P. Sloan School of Management, April 29, 1983, copy in author's possession.
6. Lawrence R. Boice and T. O. Jacobs, "Toward True Measures of Personnel Turbulence" (ARI Draft paper, Alexandria, Va., May 1988).
7. D. H. Marlowe, et al., "Unit Manning System Evaluation." Technical Report No. 1 (Washington, D.C.: Walter Reed Army Institute of Research, WRAIR,

November 1985).

8.   See U.S. Army Soldier Support Center Report, Subject: "External Turbulence Report" (Fort Benjamin Harrison, Ind., March 9, 1984), 36.

9.   Boice and Jacobs, "Toward True Measures."

10.   ARI "U.S. Army Soldier Values Survey" (Alexandria, Va.: 1987).

11.   Boice and Jacobs, "Toward True Measures," 8.

12.   Office of Deputy Chief of Staff for Personnel Briefing, "Leadership for the Nineties," for Lt. General (P) Bagnel WESTCOM, December 18, 1987.

13.   Ibid.

14.   Robert Holz, "Leadership Technical Area Report on NTC Rotation 88-5" (Alexandria, Va.: ARI, 1988).

15.   William Sanders, "Training Needs Assessment and Technology Transfer in USAREUTC" (Alexandria, Va.: ARI, 1985), 34.

16.   National Security Industrial Association Conference on Military Personnel and Training, Luxembourg, May 5, 1987.

17.   Anthony J. Quinzi, memorandum "Personnel Turbulence in a Mechanized Infantry Battalion" (APO New York 09114-5413: TRAC WSMR Field Office, October 23, 1986), 3.

18.   It was assumed that all changes could be detected by monitoring the battle roster. However, all personnel changes were not necessarily reflected on the roster.

19.   Quinzi, "Personnel Turbulence," 10–11.

20.   Ibid.

21.   Ibid. However, if the turbulence that occurred between the weekly rosters were projected as a basis for estimating actual turbulence occurring in intervals longer than two weeks, the actual median time for squad leader and gunner pairs would be six weeks.

22.   *Turbulence Definition and Measurements,* vols. 1–3. (McLean, Va.: General Research Corporation, 1982), 2–10.

23.   Ibid.

24.   Ibid., vol. 3, 3–28.

25.   Office of Deputy Chief of Staff for Personnel, Unit Manning System Division, Survey of Company Commanders and Battalion Adjutants, 1987.

6

SMALL-UNIT LEADERS
SHOULD BE WAR WINNERS

FM 100-5, the Army's field manual for combat operations, states that, more than any other factor, leadership on the battlefield will determine the outcome. This is especially true at the level of small-unit engagements. However, the ability of the U.S. Army to provide this level of combat leadership is severely limited. The exodus of NCO talent after Vietnam, reduced noncommissioned officer (NCO) authority and role confusion, reduced initiative, small numbers of quality leaders, an Enlisted Personnel Management System (EPMS) that has turned the NCO Corps away from its primary function, turbulence, and other factors in today's Army combine to degrade seriously the vital function of the NCO Corps and its ability to provide small-unit training and combat leadership.

The case for unit leadership as a prime determinant of who wins and who loses on the battlefield and the current status of small-unit leadership in the U.S. Army are outlined as follows:

- Immense firepower is concentrated in small units.
- Modern war requires dispersed, independent small-unit actions.
- Quality leadership (control) of small units is more important for winning than ever before.
- Noncommissioned officers are the primary leaders of small units.
- For institutional and policy reasons, small-unit leaders (NCOs) are not providing the quality leadership necessary to maximize the unit warfighting potential of weapons systems and the soldiers who man them.

- As a result, units in the U.S. Army are not performing to high standards and achieving the combat power necessary to win over high-performing units of opposing armies.

If the U.S. Army is to be recognized as a great army in all respects, the vital and primary function of the NCO Corps must be recognized. The single function above all others that an NCO Corps must perform in any great army and most of all in the U.S. Army is to effectively join the Army's warriors, its soldiers, to the rest of the organization; to its weapons, officers, objectives, and to the goals and values for which it is prepared to fight. U.S. Army *Field Manual 22-600-20, The Army Noncommissioned Officer Guide,* affirms this basic function of the NCO: "Sergeants must have the skill, ability, and leadership to train soldiers for combat and lead them in combat . . . fire teams, squads, crews, gun sections . . . fight together as teams, using their equipment to high standards of excellence."[1]

Evidence that the basic NCO function is not being accomplished to full effect is plentiful from a wide number of sources. In prior chapters the extremely disruptive effects of a still-pervasive turbulence were presented. Measures of ineffective bonding between small-unit leaders (primarily NCOs) and their soldiers around core professional values, the bedrock norms of any first-rate army, are presented in Chapter 7. Additional indicators of inadequate small-unit leadership are plentiful. Army exit interviews of attrittees, soldiers who quit before their first tour is completed, state, in four out of the top five reasons for leaving the Army, that small-unit leadership is the primary reason they are quitting. This is very significant. In today's "best ever" Army the overall attrition rate remains very high at 30 to 40 percent attrition during the soldier's first term.[2] Additionally, Army satisfaction surveys, the Army Experience Survey, Army values surveys, several Walter Reed Army Institute of Research (WRAIR) reports evaluating the Unit Manning System, lessons-learned reports from the National Training Center, the Leader Development Study by the Center for Army Leadership, and spot reports from top Army leaders throughout the Army all point to substantial and continuing leadership and related performance problems at the small-unit level.[3]

All of this points strongly to a major organizational fault line, a potential cleavage of significant proportions just below the surface. Given future organizational stress such as an extended inconclusive conflict in Latin America or a thirty-day or longer conventional war with a determined enemy in a European scenario, the pressures, both domestic and military, that cause an Army to unravel will become intense. For example, the weak bonding that today exists, for the most part, between U.S. combat soldiers and their immediate leaders would not survive such pressures and provide the leadership necessary to produce high-performing combat units.

The U.S. Army cannot afford to delay in fixing this organizational defect. This is not a question of the availability of NCO quality. The NCO Corps currently has much of the high quality necessary. Rather the primary issue is one of organization, management, and training policies and priorities combined with the need for a clear vision of what is needed to produce high-performing combat units and the prime role of the NCO Corps in that vision. The reason for urgency is clear. The Army has just fielded the M-1 tank and the M-2 infantry fighting vehicle, which individually and especially when combined with other systems offer the potential for unmatched conventional combat power, yet manpower, personnel, and training policies and practices severely limit the Army's ability to develop fully this enormous combat potential.

To understand why the role of the small-unit leader is more important than ever before in the history of warfare, the evolution of the recent nature of war must be understood. The effective control of soldiers in combat today is much more complex and difficult than it was even as recently as the beginning of World War II. Since the early 1940s the introduction of increasingly lethal tanks, aircraft, rifles, and machine guns supported by ever-advancing technology has tremendously increased the dispersion, confusion, chance, hardship, and danger of the modern battlefield. No longer as in past wars is the individual soldier a visible part of a large formation advancing under the watchful eyes of his chain of command to the rear. Instead, today's soldier sees himself in battle as part of a very small group or crew, represented by a few men on his right and left or in the same vehicle with a sergeant who is always near. While the trend toward larger armies with more lethal weapons, technology, and tactics has increased enormously, an opposite trend, toward much smaller, more independent, better-led, and more highly trained combat units is also apparent. These trends have increased greatly the dispersion, mobility, danger, and confusion on the modern battlefield and have made it essential that control of the individual soldier be gained through internalizing core soldier values and codes of behavior that cause the soldier to act as a reliable member of his unit in combat, especially when separated from the direct control of his leaders. Because the source of a soldier's core values and operating rules is the small group and its leaders and because the only force strong enough to make the soldier willing to face fire and advance time after time is his loyalty to the unit and the unit's expectation that he will advance, it becomes the primary task of the Army to control the small fighting group through its leaders.

Beginning after the Korean War and especially during the Vietnam War, which because of its nature was more than ever a junior leader's war, the U.S. Army recognized the greatly increased importance of the independently led small unit to battle outcomes. This change was reflected in Army doctrine as far back as 1956 when the rifle squad was divided into two fire teams with two additional sergeants to assist the squad leader as fire team leaders.[4] This change was formally institutionalized in a new field manual, *FM 7-10 Rifle Company,* which serves as an example of the Army's recognition of the increased importance of the small unit and its leaders in determining the outcome of battles. The historical changes summed up in *FM 7-10* explain:

> how the two fire team leaders assisted the squad leader in controlling the squad. They accomplished the actions directed by the squad leader, acted independently when the situation demanded it, and personally led their men in battle. The results achieved by the late 1950s reorganization can be summed up in three words: cohesion, control and maneuver. The fire teams provided a smaller primary group for soldiers and permitted natural leaders to be selected and appointed as small-unit leaders. The reorganization also provided a capability for squads composed of highly mobile, hard-hitting fire teams to conduct independent actions on the battlefield. Additionally, the two fire teams gave the squad leader the capability of maneuvering integral units under his overall command. But the primary thrust of the changes in infantry squad organization was to provide more capable small-unit leadership and to increase the importance of the Noncommissioned Officer. More effective and more numerous junior leaders provided critically needed responsiveness and flexibility at the lowest echelons.[5]

The ever-increasing importance of the small-unit leader in determining who wins and who loses at higher echelons on the battlefield was fully recognized in the latest (1986) version of *FM 100-5*:

> Wars are fought and won by men, not by machines. The human dimension of war will be decisive. . . . The fluid, compartmental nature of war will place a premium on sound leadership, competent and courageous soldiers, and cohesive, well-trained units. The conditions of combat on the next battlefield will be unforgiving of errors and will demand great skill, imagination, and flexibility of leaders.[6]

Small combat unit leadership is comprised of company grade officers, lieutenants and captains, and especially noncommissioned officers.

However, it must be recogized that the vital function of effectively linking the individual soldier to the unit is primarily an NCO function. This is so because NCOs man over 75 percent of the small-unit leadership positions and almost 100 percent of the positions that call for first-line leadership of troops in combat. Even at the company level, assigned officers have other primary duties focusing them toward coordination beyond the unit to receive orders and obtain the necessary support to achieve the mission.

The primary first-line leadership responsibility, combined with the recent development and acquisition of weapons systems such as the M-1 Abrams tank and M-2 Bradley fighting vehicle for the infantry, makes the small-unit leadership combat role of the American NCO more important than ever before. Such a role requires the most competent and resourceful leaders available.

There is no greater requirement than the need for such small-unit leadership if a nation is going to field a first-rate army and give it the edge in face-to-face battlefield engagements. The importance of this level of leadership was most recently demonstrated in 1973 in the Sinai during the Yom Kippur War. The Israeli Defense Force (IDF) was caught off guard initially on October 6 by the Egyptian forces. The IDF was reacting to an Egyptian surprise attack and there was no overall IDF battle plan. For the first week the Israeli situation was desperate.[7] The line was held by the IDF through fighting and winning hundreds of independent small-unit battles. The leadership of tank commanders and small-unit leaders was decisive and eventually allowed the IDF to mount an effective counterattack on October 14. The many separate actions that characterize the nature of the Israeli style of war and the small-unit IDF leadership upon which it rests are illustrated by an IDF tank commander who explained that when he got separated form his unit "instead of trying to locate his lost platoon . . . he chose to charge at a dozen Egyptian tanks, this being a more practical undertaking."[8] Quality leadership up front is the norm in the IDF and it is expected. The Israelis believe such leadership is dependent upon the careful process through which the IDF selects its NCOs and officers. This careful selection of small-unit leaders is the major factor in Israel's ability to produce strongly cohesive and ultimately high-performing combat units.

An explanation of the repeated defeats of Arab armies since 1948 by the IDF revolves around a major lesson to be learned by any army that desires to produce combat units capable of matching the combat performance of the best of today's armies. The combined Arab armies of millions of soldiers, drawn from a population of over 200 million people and equipped with plentiful and technologically advanced weapons systems, have been repeatedly defeated by an army of approximately 500,000 soldiers, including mobilized reserves, drawn from a population of only 3 million people, which is smaller than the population of the Washington, D.C., metropolitan area. A prime secret of the Israeli success is not really a secret but a lesson to be learned. It is the process followed by the IDF in the selection, classification, and assignment of soldiers for the IDF. The overriding consideration in this process is the search for quality soldiers and their assignment up front to key leadership positions in combat units as NOCs and later officers. This process has ensured that whenever an Israeli tank crew or small unit faces an enemy, the human element involved in the battle strongly prejudice the outcome in favor of the IDF.

The Israeli system of selection, classification, and assignment is based on extensive research on indicators of personnel quality suitable as predictors of performance in combat. This research further links "individual quality" indicators with unit performance in combat and has permitted the IDF to enhance the effective performance of units such as tank crews far above levels of performance expected on the basis of individual crew characteristics.[9]

The process through which the IDF conducts its screening to assign quality scores to soldiers is called the KABA system and has been widely described in the literature.[10] Each soldier is tested and screened before being assigned a KABA score, which indicates his soldier quality category and determines in large part his career in the IDF. In addition to intelligence and education, the KABA system measures the soldiers' motivation and categorizes them from 41 to 46 as "low quality," 47 to 50 as "moderate quality," and the top third, 51 to 56, as "high quality." Such scores and categories are arrived at through a complex and sophisticated process of interpretation that provides a highly reliable basis for predicting soldier performance in combat.[11]

The process through which the IDF validly identifies and predicts soldier performance is only half of the lesson to be learned. The lesson learned is not complete until the significance and importance of the assignment made on the basis of quality is understood. This perhaps is one of the most significant lessons the U.S. Army has yet to learn if it is to become a great army. The second half of the lesson is that the great majority within the top-third KABA category are assigned to combat units where many will become NCO leaders and some eventually officers. The moderate-category soldiers are still assigned to units in the combat area but usually in support or service roles. Clearly the system that emerges ensures that the higher the individual soldier's KABA score is, the greater the probability that he will be assigned a leadership position in a front-line combat unit.[12] In this way the Israelis achieve maximum human potential from their overall population resources. Because the human element in war is by far the most significant factor in determining the outcome of battles and eventually the war itself, any army that wants to compete on the basis of every advantage must, as a first priority, maximize its human potential in its combat units.

Superficial comparisons of manpower, personnel, and training (MPT) issues between the U.S. and Soviet armies undertaken as part of a recent competitive strategies analysis (April 1988) contained vague and ill-defined references to Soviet ethnic and cohesion problems, which led to unwarranted conclusions about Soviet weaknesses in MPT that supposedly put them at a disadvantage. Such conclusions are probably not warranted. In fact it is the U.S. Army, not the Soviet Army, that has failed to maximize the available human potential.

While the U.S. Army has only recently developed and validated predictors of performance similar to the Israeli KABA system[13] and is currently experiencing controversy about its implementation, the Soviets have had since at least the early 1980s a sophisticated testing system for selecting, classifying, and assigning soldiers based on expected performance. While the Soviets appear to incorporate political reliability into their criteria for motivational testing, there is nothing in either the Israeli or U.S. research in this area that makes the Soviet approach invalid. In fact, the high correlation between membership in approved political organizations and high quality in Soviet society probably means that the emphasis on political reliability in the Red Army leadership reinforces the placement of quality leaders throughout the Soviet Army.

It is often stated that the lack of an experienced NCO corps is a Soviet Army weakness compared to the U.S. Army.[14] This appears to be over-stated and probably indicates a lack of knowledge of the manpower and personnel policies of the two armies. In the Soviet Army the NCO Corps has a much more limited function than in the U.S. Army. The Soviet Army officer performs many of the roles assigned to the American NCO. Thus many functions at the squad and platoon level are performed by the Soviet officer corps, which is widely respected for its quality and training. Additionally, the Soviet NCO in many respects is similar to the Israeli NCO in that although young and without many years of service he is selected from among the highest quality soldiers the population has to offer and his performance in combat should be expected to reflect this quality.[15]

Contrasted with the Israeli example and probably the Soviet example as well, the U.S. Army has significant flaws that rest on the failure to maximize the human potential available and that promise to make future conflict for the U.S. Army more difficult, with an increased potential for defeat. Specifically, the MPT policies in effect today do not ensure small-unit NCO combat leaders of the highest quality. The organization in the Army that governs these policies is fragmented and without clear vision of what is necessary to provide the highest-quality leadership to combat units. Additionally, the enlisted Personnel Management System that guides NCO career paths does not reinforce the basic trainer/leader functions of the NCO Corps and encourages the highest-quality NCOs to pursue careers away from the combat arms.

The failure to provide quality leadership to U.S. combat units is rooted in the traditional American approach to war — to overwhelm our enemies with war materials provided by our huge technological and industrial superiority while safeguarding American lives. This approach is still deeply rooted in our present-day basic assumptions about defense. Implicit is the notion that American society does not have the will to provide the necessary manpower quality to defend the United States. As previously noted, the director of one of the country's largest defense agencies stated: "This society has decided that it will only use a certain fraction of its human effort in its own defense. . . . We are what we are. We don't have the resolve . . . that's it."[16]

It must be recognized that this traditional American approach to war is no longer feasible, especially during the first days and months of a conventional war in Europe or elsewhere. During this period the United States would not have superiority in quantity of war materials, weapons, or personnel, and superiority in warfighting technology would be mixed at best.

Also not recognized is the fact that the U.S. Army would be seriously outclassed in the human element of warfighting, especially in small-unit leadership, which is identified in the Army's premier how-to-fight manual, *FM 100-5,* as the most critical of all factors affecting who wins and loses on the battlefield.

This is a significant shortcoming. The United States has never before faced a strategic situation in which the importance of modern conventional warfare is increasing because of nuclear arms control agreements while at the same time being outnumbered in conventional materials, weapons, and personnel in an operational setting that makes independent, aggressive, and smart leadership on the battlefield more important than ever before in the history of war. As discussed earlier, the increased chance, danger, confusion, complexity, and dispersion of modern warfare have all greatly affected the role and the importance of the small-unit leader, especially the first-line NCO directly charged with leading troops into combat. Without the best leadership possible at this level, the other strengths of the United States such as its tremendous productivity and innovative technology will not be successfully brought to bear. Small-unit leadership will be especially important in the first thirty days of war where enormous advantages can be won and the final outcome determined.

The importance of high-quality small-unit combat leaders to success on the battlefield has been presented in a historical study conducted at the U.S. Military Academy. It found that successful small unit leaders had a "particular facility for planning in detail, assessing a changing situation, and continually assimilating large quantities of often conflicting data. Facility in this regard appears to be a function of intelligence, experience, and moral courage."[17]

The strong association of high-quality soldiers and performance with intelligence has been repeatedly demonstrated by researchers.[18] The U.S. Army has most recently confirmed the Israeli experience and demonstrated a strong association between soldier quality defined in terms of intelligence and soldier performance in a major research project, Project A.[19] The strength of this relationship is demonstrated in Table 6.1, which shows the relationship of soldier performance in core infantry tasks with mental ability measured by AFQT.[20]

Such a relationship is even more critical to the performance of small-unit leaders. The need for accurate and complex planning and the requirement to assess rapidly changing situations and assimilate large amounts of seemingly unrelated data in combat require the highest-quality leaders available.

Unfortunately, the U.S. Army for the most part does not have this quality of small-unit leadership assigned as infantry squad leaders, tank commanders, artillery section chiefs, and platoon sergeants. This is critical. This is the primary level of unit leadership. It is at this level that the individual is either made a fully effective soldier fighting as part of a high-performing unit or is lost to the Army because of ineffective leadership.

Almost as critical is the fact that small-unit NCOs will be the primary source of company-level officer replacements during the first thirty days of war. Casualty rates in a conventional war scenario in Europe, for

TABLE 6.1
Soldier Performance by AFQT for Core Infantry Tasks
(MOS Code = 11B)

PERFORMANCE

Frequency Row Pct		Low 1/3	Mid 1/3	Top 1/3	Total
	I	4 11.76	7 20.59	23 67.65	34
	II	26 18.44	43 30.50	72 51.06	141
AFQT	IIIA	31 31.63	41 41.84	26 26.53	98
	IIIB	58 38.16	56 36.84	38 25.00	152
	IVA	45 68.18	17 25.76	4 6.06	66
	TOTAL	164	164	163	491

SOURCE: ARI: PROJECT A

example, are expected to be very high, especially for officers such as platoon leaders and company commanders. There is no other immediate source to replace these officers other than from the NCO ranks and it is essential that these replacements be of the highest quality.

The next two chapters support in detail that the U.S. Army does not have the quality small-unit NCO leadership required in the combat branches and this significantly affects Army warfighting capabilities. On the average, quality measures of combat-unit NCO leaders show that only about 25 percent are in the top one-third. One large combat military occupational specialty (MOS) has only 10 percent in the top one-third. In most combat arms branches, the great majority of small-unit leaders, approximately 50 to 60 percent, are in the bottom half when measured for quality. Even more discouraging is the fact that only about half of this already small number of top-quality combat leaders or about 13 percent of all combat NCOs are assigned to combat units even though their MOS indicates this is where their duty assignments should be. This is in sharp contrast to the Israeli defense forces, which as a matter of policy ensure that almost all of their small-unit leaders are from the top one-third in quality. It must be stressed that this is not an issue of minorities. Quality small-unit leaders are available in all of the minorities represented in today's Army. Rather, it appears to be an issue of organizational inertia and tradition.

Specific examination of the quality of infantry and armor small-unit leaders is especially discouraging when it is realized that the successful employment of the M-1 Abrams tank and the M-2 Bradley fighting vehicle is largely dependent on NCO abilities.

The dearth of quality leaders available to combat units is examined in Chapters 7 and 8. It is sufficient here to point out that the quality NCOs assigned as tank commanders, squad leaders, M-2 infantry fighting vehicle commanders, and other key small-unit combat leadership positions cannot begin to fill necessary leadership requirements.

The requirements placed on the leaders of the M-1 and M-2 in order successfully to engage and defeat a like capability in an opposing army are enormous, and to ensure that U.S. units win these small-unit engagements there can be no substitute for top-quality leadership at this level. This is especially true today given reports of Soviet technologically superior armor force as well as their greatly superior numbers and the high probability that their tank crews are carefully selected to provide high-quality crews.[21]

The duties of M-1 tank commanders or M-2 infantry fighting vehicle commanders are complex. These systems fill out the combined arms team on the battlefield and in many respects are much more complex systems for the staff sergeants who will command them. In addition to the high technology in the cupolas that must be mastered, the nature of the Bradley's role on the battlefield requires that its leader be capable of assessing rapidly changing situations and processing large amounts of often conflicting information, as well as being capable of leading a dismounted infantry squad. There is significant concern in elements of the Army's MANPRINT community that the fast-paced nature of combined arms operations will fully task-load even the highest-quality and well-trained commanders and crews of the Abrams M-1 and the Bradley M-2.[22]

Conversations with those responsible for evaluating these systems with soldiers and commander included as part of the system reflect significant concerns that for the most part, armor and infantry NCOs currently assigned to these systems, as well as some lieutenants, "lack the aptitude to fully exploit the full potential" of the basic M-1 and M-2 systems.[23] Even more concern is expressed when advanced technological modifications already under way in these systems are discussed. For example, the tank or vehicle commander, usually in the NCO grade of staff sergeant (E-6), will have to operate the new position-navigation (POS/NAV) system, the tank commander's independent thermal sight (CITS), the smoke system (CUDOS), and other systems such as the tank commander's battle management system (BMS), which could on occasion require all of his attention as it can provide the most accurate information about enemy and friendly forces on the immediate battlefield. The specific concern mentioned was that an overall NCO population already marginally qualified with limited ability to keep up with the current systems will be even less capable of exploiting and achieving full battlefield advantage from the even more advanced systems. Again, it was stressed that the issue was not whether they could learn to operate such systems even in a fair to middling manner, but whether the assigned small-unit leaders are capable of maximizing the potential of such systems and combining such abilities with the initiative and judgment required of leaders to win on today's battlefields.

Most of the small number of top-quality combat arms NCOs are not actually assigned to small-unit troop-leading positions.[24] For example, quality NCOs are required to fill recruiting positions in Recruiting Command, drill sergeant positions in various training commands, and many other administrative or support positions. Thousands of NCO noncombat leader positions are filled by NCO combat leaders who are screened to ensure that only quality NCOs are selected for noncombat positions that contribute little to warfighting. The extent of this practice and the dearth of quality NCOs in combat leadership positions are reflected in NCO promotion statistics over the past several years. For example, a recent board for promotions to sergeant E-7 from staff sergeant E-6 had widely varying promotion rates depending upon assignment. It is well known, for example, that the Recruiting Command accepts only high-quality NCOs among its approximately 8,000 NCOs and the promotion board results reflect this NCO assignment policy. The USAREC selection rate to sergeant E-7 was 97 percent while the overall Army selection rate was only 17 percent.[25] Cause for concern still is the extremely low promotion rate for those NCOs in small-unit combat leader positions, which has been only around 10 percent.[26]

To the extent that the problem of insufficient quality in small-unit leadership positions is recognized, it is often commented that the increase in quality junior soldiers (E-1 and E-4) over the past several years will eventually result in higher quality combat leaders as more quality soldiers reenlist for careers as NCOs. This is an unrealistic expectation as it would require reenlistment of high-quality soldiers at an extraordinary rate — something that we should not expect as we attract them initially into the Army with bonuses and promises that are usually fully realizable only by leaving the Army (e.g., college bonus). At any rate, this expectation does not appear to be achieving even moderate realization. Reenlistment of quality first-term soldiers (E-1 through E-4) continues to be low and current rates offer little encouragement. From 1985 to 1988, in spite of a conscious effort, the Army was only able to raise the overall quality among the top one-third of its E-5 NCOs by 24 percent and E-6 NCOs by 12 percent.[27] As noted earlier, for example, this resulted in the Army achieving a strength of about 396 quality E-6s on MOS 19K, M-1 tank commanders.

In examining the determinants of first-term soldiers' decision to reenlist or leave the Army it was found that the single major determinant was the soldiers' organizational commitment.[28] The inability of current unit leaders to bond their soldiers to the organization, as discussed in the next chapter, is reflected in the current weakness in organizational commitment among quality first termers and their decision, for the great majority, not to reenlist.

The problem of too few quality NCOs as small-unit leaders is further compounded by malassignment of the precious few to noncombat positions from which they cannot contribute their combat skills in the critical early days of any future war. The time required for such leaders to form cohesive units based on trust and mutual respect will not be available under current organizations and policies. If this persists, some of the U.S. Army's darkest days are bound to be repeated. The history of the Thirty-sixth Infantry Division in World War II is a prime example. The Thirty-sixth Division spearheaded the invasion of southern France from Italy in 1944 with an attack across the Rapido River south of Rome. The division lost 2,200 men in two days. The greatest single cause was the lack of cohesion. Leaders were given substantial numbers of individual replacements just prior to the battle and small units entered combat as units of strangers not knowing their leaders and fellow soldiers.

The thought that many high-quality NCOs currently filling noncombat positions could be reassigned in the event of war would lead to low performance on the battlefield and set conditions for a repeat of the battle of Rapido River. Those under the impression that the buildup of forces during World War II was a smooth and patriotic process that can serve as a model should read the recently declassified Secret October 1941 Memorandum to General Marshall from Lieutenant General McNair. So rocky were the training and leadership problems encountered during mobilization in 1941 that General McNair recommended demobilization of several divisions until the "astounding" and "shocking state" of discipline could be corrected and "competent leaders [could] straighten out matters."[29]

The Army must begin to provide and maintain quality small-unit leadership. The problem of inadequate numbers of top-quality NCOs in small-unit combat positions is not unsurmountable. Further, it is not a question of minority underrepresentation among top-quality NCOs. The Army currently has approximately 54,000 NCOs in the grades E-5 and E-6 that rank in the top one-third measure of quality. Minorities are proportionately represented in this number.

The question of why the Army can't provide top-quality leaders for its crucial combat units becomes even more pointed. The effect of this failure to provide the necessary priority to small-unit leadership is made clear in the next chapters, which make clear the higher standards of performance necessary to win in war.

NOTES

1. Department of the Army, PM 22-600-20, *The Army Non Commissioned Officer Guide* (Washington, D.C.: Government Printing Office, 1980), 2–5.
2. Army Exit Interviews in Issues Briefing for Deputy Chief of Staff for Personnel, U.S. Army, May 27, 1986. A soldier's first term can be from two to four years, depending on his contract.

3. Small-unit leadership was not the specific focus of any of these reports; therefore, it is noteworthy that each report has significant comment or data on this issue.

4. U.S. Military Academy, "The Quality of the Army's Non-Commissioned Officer" (West Point, N.Y.: United States Military Academy, History Department, unpublished paper), 6.

5. Ibid., 6.

6. Department of the Army Field Manual 100–5, *Operations* (Washington, D.C.: Government Printing Office, 1986), 5.

7. Reuven Gal, *The Israeli Soldier* (Westport, Conn.: Greenwood Press, 1987), 21.

8. Samuel Rolbant, *The Israeli Soldier: Profile of an Army* (Cranbury, N.J.: Thomas Yoseloff, 1970).

9. The Israeli defense forces, especially the psychological testing branch and the classification branch, have sponsored research for years that indicates there is a highly stable, reliable, and validated predictive index between psychological test scores and performance in combat. These data are very similar to U.S. Army Project A data described in Chapter 3. See Francis C. Grafton, Darlene M. Olson, Newell Kent Eaton, and Lawrence M. Hanser, *Project A Concurrent Validation Results* and briefing "The Army's Project A — Improving Selection, Classification and Utilization of Army Enlisted Personnel," (Alexandria, Va.: Army Research Institute, 1987).

10. Gal, *The Israeli Soldier*, 94–95.

11. Ibid., 79–80.

12. Ibid., 80–81.

13. Project A is a long-range research and development effort undertaken by the Manpower Research Laboratory of the Army Research Institute. Its purpose is to identify those soldiers most capable of performing well through selection and classification tests; it has developed a highly predictive, reliable, and valid index of test scores and performance.

14. V. V. Shelyag, A. D. Glotochkin, and K. K. Platonov, "Military Psychology: A Soviet View" (Moscow: 1972), translated and published by the U.S. Air Force, 303.

15. The Soviet Army doesn't rely on its NCO Corps for in-depth technical knowledge and experience for its support and service functions. These roles are usually performed by officers, warrant officers, and technical sergeants.

16. Robert Cooper, in Michael Schrage, "The Sword of Science," *Washington Post Magazine,* October 9, 1983, 22–23.

17. Kenneth E. Hamburger, "Leadership in Combat: An Historical Appraisal" (West Point, N.Y.: U.S. Military Academy, Department of History, 1981), 3.

18. See, for example, data produced by the U.S. Army Recruiting Command's Juri Toomipuu.

19. Grafton, et al., *Project A,* Linking Soldier Quality to Combat Performance.

20. Ibid.

21. Phillip A. Karber, Center for Strategic and International Affairs, Testimony to Senate Armed Services Committee, November 3, 1987.

22. MANPRINT stands for Manpower and Personnel Integration and is concerned with the total system capability that results when individual soldier and crew performance is evaluated as part of the overall system.

23. Such evaluations must fully task-load the system crew and commander. This overload is not evident in some much-heralded tank gunner tables and results. Such evaluations do not provide adequate and valid tests of the crew and weapon.

24. Department of Defense Manpower Data Center, (DMDC) data base, May 1988.

25. "NCO Promotions," *Recruiter Journal* (U.S. Army Recruiting Command) 41, no. 5 (March 11, 1988): 1.

26. "Here's How E-7 Stripes Fell by MOS," *Army Times,* February 9, 1987, 1.

27. DMDC, data base.

28. Alfred L. Smith, Jr., "A Multivariate Analysis of Determinants Reenlistment: A Decision-Making Model for Enlisted Personnel," ARI working paper, March 1988.

29. L. J. McNair, Memorandum for General Marshall, Subject: Railey Investigation, General Headquarters, U.S. Army, October 14, 1941.

7

WHY CAN'T THE AMERICAN ARMY CREATE COHESIVE UNITS?

Modern warfighting requires that the soldier be alone except for two or three fellow soldiers on his right, left, or in his vehicle or the next vehicle. Control of soldiers either in a modern European or Third World scenario presents major leadership problems for any army. The significance of the small unit to which the soldier belongs can hardly be overstated when considering leadership in war.

The immense advantages in warfighting that accrue to an army that fields highly motivated soldiers fighting under superb small-unit leaders can be measured through the concept of cohesion. This chapter presents the broad requisites for cohesion and reviews the inability of the U.S. Army to produce cohesive units.

- Core soldier values formed by their immediate leaders are primary determinants of the soldiers' day-to-day actions in high-performing units.
- Cohesion measures reflect the degree of soldier bonding to each other and to unit leaders as well as soldier and unit commitment to core values and the goals for which they fight.
- Measures of soldier core values and bonding to unit and leaders strongly indicate the U.S. Army has been unable to reach out to today's quality soldiers and bond them to their units and to the Army.
- Indicators of cohesion, initially high after basic training, fall off sharply after assignment to the regular Army and continue to drop thereafter.
- Soldier views of immediate unit leaders (E-5 through E-7) indicate a severe shortcoming in leaders' adherence to core professional values.

- The Cohesion, Operational Readiness and Training (COHORT) program does not produce cohesive units and as implemented has been largely ineffective.
- The Army is no closer today to achieving cohesive units than it was in 1980. This comparative lack of cohesion would be a significant weakness in combat against other more cohesive armies.

Through effective leadership, the small group develops strong professional values that serve as the basis of dominant rules of behavior within the small unit. Over time these rules form expectations among the members of a unit about their individual conduct and in a strongly cohesive unit they become the primary determinant of the soldier's behavior, especially in the danger, uncertainty, stress, and confusion of modern war. In a unit with strong leadership, all other influences on the soldier's behavior become secondary and the soldier adheres to a set of core soldier values. Such core values are common in any first-rate army. Fighting skill, professional teamwork, physical stamina, self-discipline, duty (selfless service), respect for unit leaders (both professionally and personally), and loyalty to unit are core soldier values common to all first-rate armies. The presence and strength of core soldier values and their relationship to a unit's warfighting capability are direct and measurable.

The measurement of soldier and unit values that reflect the individual soldier's commitment to his leaders and unit is currently best accomplished as a portion of the overall measurement of unit cohesion. As previously discussed, such measures assess the bonding among members of a unit (horizontal bonding), the influence of the leader on the small group (vertical bonding), and the resulting individual and group commitment to core values that bind a soldier to his unit and the goals for which it fights.[1] In many respects measures of a unit's core professional values are the most significant for assessing a unit's warfighting capability. While such measures are dependent upon horizontal and vertical bonding, core soldier values are a valid indicator of a soldier's willingness to follow his unit leaders in pursuit of Army objectives.

Current assessments of cohesion in the U.S. Army give sufficient doubt to claims that this is the best Army ever. Various assessments over recent years give adequate basis for questioning such claims.[2] An overall assessment must include the deleterious effects of turbulence on horizontal bonding; the inability of small-unit leaders, primarily because of system faults, to gain predominance in small units; and the resulting inability of small units to grow and fully develop strong professional core values expected of any first-rate army. Until basic systemic and policy defects in each of these areas are corrected, the U.S. Army will not rise above an army of average human capability. If, as one often hears, the Army is people and what it accomplishes or fails to accomplish is thus dependent upon people, the harnessing of human potential rather than weapons and systems development is currently the greatest challenge facing today's U.S. Army.

This task is traditionally the most difficult for the U.S. Army to deal with. As outlined previously, of the four broad elements that comprise any nation's defense posture — weapons and technology, logistics, force structure, and strategy — it is force structure or maximizing the human potential available in the U.S. population that has traditionally presented the greatest difficulty for the United States. While expensive, controversial, and sometimes suspect, the acquisition of high-performance weapons systems and their supporting logistics has successfully developed a very strong constituency within the defense industry. Shrewd placement of these industries throughout the United States makes most congressmen enthusiastic supporters of at least a portion of the defense industry. Likewise strategic thought has built up a strong and well-known constituency located mainly in university and think tank communities. Force structure, however, in terms of manpower, personnel, and training (MPT) issues, has no widespread constituency anywhere outside of the Army. This issue has no industry dependent upon it as do the research, development, and acquisition of weapons systems. Congress has no incentive to deal with force structure issues. The resolution of these issues often is too painful and expensive with no direct beneficiary. Therefore, MPT issues lag and somehow never seem to bubble to the top for resolution until they become significantly out of adjustment and worrisome.

Now, two major changes require that manpower, personnel, and training issues be addressed. The first change is the widely noted and increased strategic significance of conventional ground forces discussed in Chapter 2. The overriding need for more effective forces, both active Army and reserve forces, is going to raise force structure issues and require painful decisions. The second major factor is the recent availability of compelling research data in the manpower, personnel, and training areas that unmask significant and widespread inefficiencies in current Army organization and policies that severely and adversely affect training, unit performance, and warfighting capability. Most compelling, however, is the emergence of data that show significant efficiencies are possible in personnel organization and utilization that make possible marked increases in the Army's warfighting capacity.

The availability of data from across the Army on core professional values and cohesion is an example. These data point to significant systemic shortcomings affecting small-unit performance. When combined with other similar data on manpower, personnel, and training issues, they point up wider significant patterns of systemic shortcomings.[3] As indicated earlier, a pattern of evidence pointing to a systemic failure of small-unit leadership has become evident. It involves the inability of small-unit leaders to become fully effective leaders and create cohesive, high-performing units capable of matching the overall human potential developed by other first-rate armies. Much of what the U.S. Army does in this area compares well to that in the best armies worldwide. The quality of its junior officers and soldiers and the training, technology, and weapons provided its units for the most part are very competitive. The weaknesses that prevent the full development and application of the human potential available to the U.S. Army are to be found in its force structure and organizational policies, especially those affecting manpower, personnel, and training issues.

To understand this, it is necessary to review the evidence in a continuous stream that begins with the soldier's decision to enlist and continues through his training, assignment to his first and subsequent units, and finally to his early attrition, or his decision to reenlist or not reenlist.

Figure 7.1 makes it clear that presently quality volunteers from the U.S. Army do not enlist primarily to serve for patriotic reasons and such motivation is not a dominating force in the soldier's first tour of duty. The figure shows that the great majority of soldiers enlisted on the basis of an economic calculation. In fact, one of the most popular economic attractions was a combined package that allowed male high school graduates to enlist for the shortest time possible (two years) for a job (usually combat arms) with a college fund bonus waiting for them at the end of two years. It also provided an economic incentive to attract them out of the Army just as it attracted them into the Army.

Although it is clear that "economic man" motivation initially attracts the great majority of volunteers to the Army, it does not necessarily mean that economic man motivation must continue as the prime motivator once a recruit is in the Army. History shows that cohesive units can be created no matter how the recruit was induced into an army. Even armies formed through press gangs or the harshest type of draft have been able to maximize the human potential and create cohesive and high-performing

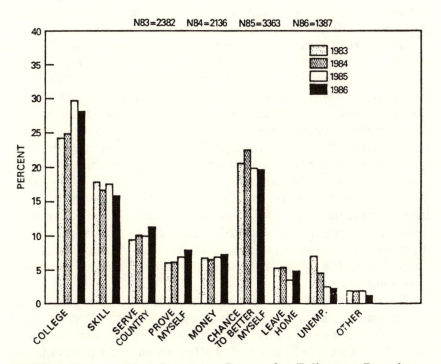

FIGURE 7.1 — Most Important Reason for Enlistment Recruits — High School Graduates — Top Half Mental Category

units.[4] Unfortunately, most combat units in today's U.S. Army are not able to accomplish this and are not able to match the human performance of first-rate armies. This reflects the conscious decision noted by Charles Moskos that top Army leaders have opted for the occupational model rather than the service ethic characteristic of an institutional model.[5]

Even though the decision of today's U.S. soldier to enlist is based on economic motivation, the American recruit comes on active duty eagerly. Survey and interview data show he is eager to develop personally, to mature and learn, to become "all that he can become." During basic training it is evident that this new recruit, the developing soldier, is open to joining the Army both physically and mentally. The attraction is the challenge of the initial training and its demand that the new soldier learn and mature in response to the leadership and high-quality training presented in basic training. Indicators of cohesion in basic training are invariably high. The attraction of the unit and its leadership become the dominant factor in the soldier's life. No other factor (e.g., family, money, old friends) can match the norms of the unit in controlling the new soldier's day-to-day behavior. His personal operating rules reflect the highest core soldier values: professional skill, teamwork, physical stamina, self-discipline, duty, loyalty to unit, and respect for unit leaders.

All of this comes to an abrupt end at the finish of the soldier's initial entry training. Without any attempt to preserve the great enthusiasm developed by most basic training graduates for the Army and their immediate leaders, the Army fragments the tremendously powerful units it has created. The trainee graduates are sent off as individual replacements or as part of a small group package replacement system that promises to be little better than an individual replacement system. The effect of this on the core professional values acquired by the trainee graduate upon which the Army has just spent enormous resources in dollars and leadership is immediate and immensely discouraging. Numerous studies and research reflect this abrupt discontinuity. The results of one of the most recent research efforts are shown in Figure 7.2.

Figure 7.2 represents the change in the American soldier's (E-1 to E-4) professional core values as he progresses through initial training and through his first tour of duty, which is all the military duty most will have. The figure shows that within a few months of reporting to the soldier's first unit the soldier's adherence to core soldier values drops 20 percent. Further study indicates these core soldier values will continue to drop significantly throughout the soldier's first tour. This is reflected by measures of cohesion that approach and sometimes reach below midscale and are definite indicators that the Army has not created fully cohesive units, but lags around the average or below average marks in this vital indicator of unit performance in combat.[6]

The sharp drop of about 20 percent in the importance of core soldier values to the American soldier after joining his first unit is tempered a little by relatively higher measures of the individual soldier core value of professional skill. This core value is maintained relatively higher throughout the soldier's career and reflects the soldier's confidence in his individual skills. Most troubling for the Army are sharp drops in measures indicating the soldier is not strongly bonded to his unit and his leaders, and thus to the Army and its objectives. For example, only about one-third of the first-term soldiers in combat units considered the core soldier values of loyalty to their unit or duty in the sense of "selfless service" to be important core values that should govern their day-to-day behavior as soldiers.[7]

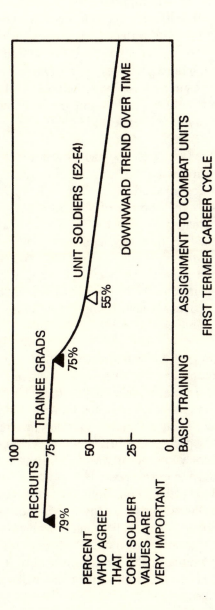

FIGURE 7.2 — Core Soldier Values (*Note:* Downward Trend after 55 percent drop is based on data reflected in Figures 3.2 and 4.2.
Source: ARI Soldier Values Survey Briefing 1987)

113

More focused looks at indicators of cohesion over time strongly support the reports of dissipation and erosion of core soldier values. Examination in Figure 7.3 of cohesion indicators at two points in the life of several COHORT units reflects sharp decreases in cohesion. From time one when the unit was new and comprised of first-term soldiers who were recent trainee graduates to time two was approximately twelve months. Both measures are for the same units. It should be noted that the trend is down toward the scale midpoint or below indicating a strongly decreasing ability of unit leaders to influence their soldiers over time.[8]

The inability of the Army to use the power of cohesion to its advantage and allow it to match the human capability of other world-class armies is further documented by the Walter Reed Army Institute of Research (WRAIR).[9] The purpose of the COHORT system was to capture the power of small-unit cohesion for the combat units of the U.S. Army. We expected significantly increased combat effectiveness and high unit performance through the "singular focus, dedication, motivation, commitment, and proficiency" of the U.S. soldier to his leaders, his unit, and the mission.[10] The inability of the Army to achieve this degree of unit effectiveness and to implement so much of what is known about how to create cohesive units is further shown in Figures 7.4 and 7.5.

In an intense study of four different COHORT battalions, major indicators of cohesion showed a marked and significant decline over time. First measured in September 1985, these indicators were significantly lower when measured the second time in June 1986.[11] The measure of horizontal cohesion in Figure 7.4 reflects this trend; however, as WRAIR researchers point out, interviews of soldiers still show significant horizontal cohesion, but it was more limited and carefully extended toward selected and trusted peers.[12]

The decline in the vertical cohesion measures are even more important. They reveal the Army's inability to reach out to a group of highly motivated, intelligent young soldiers and bring them into the Army in a manner that makes them highly committed and disciplined soldiers in cohesive units who are willing to give their "primary loyalty to the group so that it trains and fights as a unit with all members willing to risk death to achieve a common objective."[13]

At the worst end of this trend were some units that were not far from a situation of complete alienation between soldiers and their leaders. The

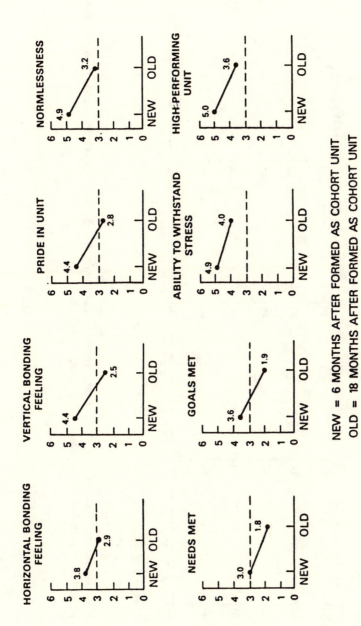

FIGURE 7.3 — Cohesion Indicators (E1–E4) (*Source:* Values Survey 1986)

NEW = 6 MONTHS AFTER FORMED AS COHORT UNIT
OLD = 18 MONTHS AFTER FORMED AS COHORT UNIT

115

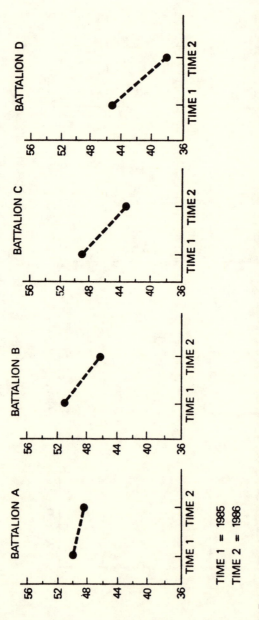

FIGURE 7.4 — Horizontal Cohesion in Four Light Infantry Battalions for Soldiers in Grades E-1 through E-4 (*Note*: Scores range from 0 to 100 with a scale mean of 50. *Source*: WRAIR Tech Rpt No. 5)

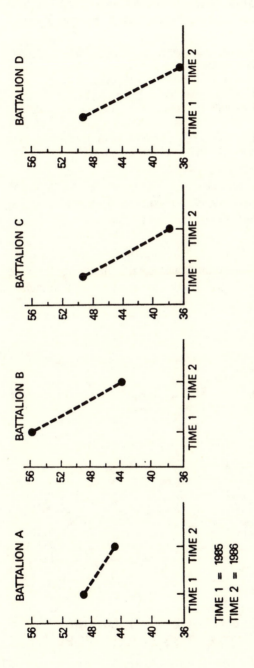

FIGURE 7.5 — Vertical Cohesion in Four Light Infantry Battalions for Soldiers in Grades E-1 through E-4 (*Note:* Scores range from 0 to 100 with a scale mean of 50. *Source:* WRAIR Tech Rpt No. 5)

TIME 1 = 1985
TIME 2 = 1986

significant lack of vertical cohesion in such COHORT units is reflected in the following recounting of an incident on a long march:

> *Private No. 1:* "F___ it, I ain't going to carry this mother-f___ machine gun no more." (Throws it on the ground.)
> *Sergeant:* "Just leave it there. Someone will pick it up."
> *Private No. 2:* "Not me. I carried the f___ yesterday."
> *Private No. 3:* "Like hell. You only carried it on the flat. I carried it up the f___ hill."
> *Sergeant:* "Somebody better f___ pick it up, or I'll kick somebody's ass."
> *Private No. 4:* (muttered) "Bull shit."[14]

More frequent indicators of the absence of vertical cohesion were defensive comments by unit members to the effect that higher-up echelons did not "share their values and priorities and were indifferent to their needs."[15]

These findings from battalions provide a close look at the Army's attempt to build cohesive units and are not unique to these four battalions alone. Figure 7.6 reflects Army-wide measures and indicates the problem

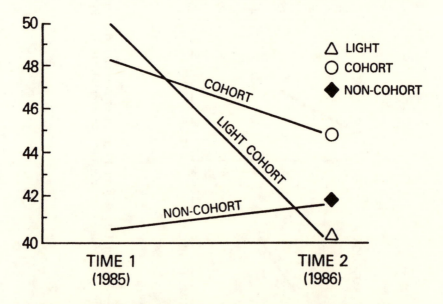

THE POSSIBLE RANGE OF SCORES ON THIS SCALE IS FROM 0 TO 100. THE SCALE MIDPOINT IS 50.

FIGURE 7.6 — **Vertical Cohesion Survey Data** (*Source:* WRAIR Tech Rept No. 5)

is pervasive throughout the Army.[16] It should be noted that while the COHORT units declined significantly in leadership effectiveness, non-COHORT units, while not declining in vertical cohesion, maintained a consistently low measure of vertical bonding well below the scale mid-point and the initial heights achieved by the COHORT units.

Specific content about the nature of the vertical bonding between small-unit leaders and their soldiers is available through a recent survey of U.S. combat units in the United States and in Europe. The findings of this research indicate that strong core soldier values are a function of leadership. Those soldiers who were closely bonded to their unit leaders reflected their leaders' professional values and reported that core soldier values were very or extremely important to them.[17] Unfortunately, this degree of vertical bonding was not widespread. Instead, as Figure 7.7 shows, most soldiers saw their immediate leaders as giving little

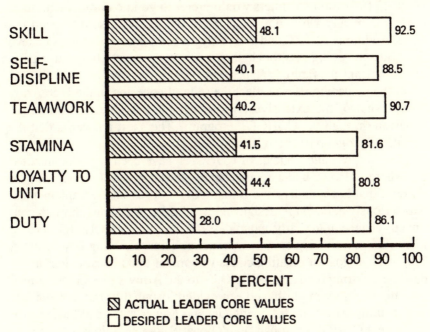

FIGURE 7.7 — Shortfall between Combat Unit Soldiers' (E1–E4) View of Their Leaders' (E5–E7) Actual Adherence to Core Professional Values and Soldiers' View of Desired Leader Adherence to Core Values (*Source:* ARI Values Survey)

importance to core soldier values and thus offering little basis for positive professional bonding between soldiers and leaders.

The significance of all of this for the U.S. Army is potentially overwhelming but not widely recognized. These measures offer valid indicators of the Army's cohesive posture and warfighting ability without the test of combat and raise the question that has been previously and so aptly put by many. It asks "Why is our Army seemingly incapable of learning?"[18] There are also in existence comparative and worrisome findings from a variety of sources about how the U.S. Army compares in its ability to mobilize the human potential of the American people with that of other armies (e.g., Australian, Israeli, Vietnamese, and Soviet).

A brief illustration is provided by a comparison of cohesiveness between Australian and U.S. Army combat units commissioned by the Deputy Chief of Staff for personnel in April 1987. The findings were not reassuring. The Australian researcher, after surveying U.S. combat units, concluded that "Australian units are more cohesive" on the basis that 77 percent of Australian soldiers would prefer to go into combat with their present company while only 33 percent of American soldiers said the same. Additionally, he found that "only 15 percent of Australians believe that when the going gets tough, their company seems to fall apart easily. For Americans the figure is 40 percent."[19]

If the preceding pages reflect the state of cohesion in the U.S. Army today, what of the extensive efforts over the past decade to improve cohesion through the COHORT program? The short answer is that the COHORT program has been largely ineffective.

The purpose and policies of COHORT have been well documented elsewhere and were understood generally, if not in detail, throughout the Army. What is not understood is that COHORT, as finally implemented, was seriously deficient in design and was further weakened through continuous change in the early and mid-1980s. Eventually COHORT became identified as a shifting set of personnel policies, affecting first-termers. The original goal of creating cohesive combat units became lost in the day-to-day struggle to adapt COHORT to the Army's existing personnel system. The goal might have been evident originally, but became lost over a number of years following General Meyer's original guidance to implement COHORT through "evolutionary, not revolutionary" changes. Unfortunately, as time progressed, action officers changed, priorities shifted, and the ongoing system with its inertia absorbed, alleviated, and neutralized the purposes of the COHORT program.

As early as spring 1986, it was apparent that COHORT was in serious difficulty. Not even 10 percent of the Army's combat units had been converted to COHORT and even this was straining the Army's personnel replacement system. As a result even this low percentage is now eroding.[20] On the basis of measurements of COHORT versus non-COHORT units that showed little difference between the two types of units, many who had earlier remained silent began to express doubts. The Army's Deputy Chief of Staff for Personnel stated that measurements by TRADOC and a recent Inspector General report cited measurements that did not support the COHORT program.[21] Further, the Under Secretary of the Army in 1987 reportedly stated that future war will require that the U.S. Army rely on making up units and crews at the last minute and that the personnel system couldn't keep units together, therefore we shouldn't expect COHORT to do so now.

Underlying this and other widespread doubt and criticism of COHORT, especially among many members of the Army's personnel community, were questionable measurements of COHORT effectiveness as well as a desire to protect the individual replacement system around which an enormous and vested Army bureaucracy has developed.

Such attitudes and the measurements of COHORT effectiveness upon which they were based are not valid. The measurements as conducted by the Combined Arms Test Activity at Fort Hood, Texas, were wrong for two reasons. First, the behavior chosen for measurement to reflect cohesion was inappropriate. Second, such measures were based on the assumption that the COHORT program as structured did in fact produce cohesive units. Unrecognized was the fact that serious flaws in the design and implementation of COHORT precluded significant improvements in cohesion. Therefore there was little cohesion present for measurement.

First, the measurements chosen, such as reenlistment rates, weapons status, and logistical indicators in COHORT units, were not appropriate measures. For example, comparing reenlistment rates for COHORT and non-COHORT units is not a valid measure. The assumption behind this measurement was that COHORT soldiers, being more committed to their unit, would reenlist at markedly higher rates than other soldiers. However, frequent measures showed there was not much difference in reenlistment rates between COHORT and non-COHORT units. These measurements have frequently been cited as proof that COHORT isn't producing units with more cohesion and therefore is not worth the effort and cost.

Such measurements are not valid indicators of the U.S. Army's ability to produce cohesive units. For example, we shouldn't be surprised that members of COHORT units don't reenlist. We told COHORT soldiers from almost their first day in the Army that they would be together three years and their unit would then "disestablish." For the next three years their closest companions would be in their unit, then it was programmed to disappear and they would move on to pursue college with their college benefits or new skills acquired in the Army. In other words, the Army recruited many of these soldiers with promised benefits that could be realized only by leaving the Army and then created and reinforced throughout the soldier's first tour the expectation that their primary connection with the Army, their COHORT unit, would cease to exist after their first tour of duty. Given these expectations in COHORT units, why would we expect higher reenlistment rates in these units?

Other measurements point up even greater flaws in the design of the COHORT program. For example, analysis of comparative measurements of weapons loss rates and logistical consumption figures starts with the basic assumption that COHORT soldiers would naturally respect Army values and goals that safeguarded weapons, conserved gasoline and other supplies, and so on, and that these norms would be reflected in contrasting measurements with weaker norms in non-COHORT units. Again there was little difference in these measurements between COHORT and non-COHORT units. This led many to conclude there was little support for the assumption that COHORT units have stronger norms that promote Army values and goals.

These measurements demonstrate a major flaw in the evaluation of COHORT. It was assumed that COHORT was synonymous with cohesion. Therefore measurements of COHORT units were considered the same as measuring cohesion. By itself, COHORT could not produce cohesion. COHORT, when finally implemented, became merely a set of personnel policies with the primary purpose of bringing assignment stability to first-term soldiers. Its main effect has been to bring about a marginal decrease in personnel turbulence among first-termers with a corresponding slight increase in horizontal bonding among some first-termers. However, as discussed in Chapter 5, even these policies, designed to decrease personnel turbulence, were marginally successful because of their implementation at only the battalion level and not within smaller units, which is necessary in order to effect stability between the soldier and his immediate leaders. Ignored was the knowledge that much more is required to produce cohesive units: strong vertical bonding between soldiers and leaders primarily at the NCO levels, as well as the building of congruent values and operating rules (norms) between soldiers, leaders, and the Army. These requisites for building cohesive units were not addressed within the COHORT and New Manning systems. They must be addressed through specific policies if the U.S. Army is going to form and maintain cohesive units.

In mid-1989, the COHORT program as previously marketed within the Army and still currently thought of, as a battalion-level program, was no longer in existence. Currently the Army staff, especially the personnel managers, are cutting and pasting in an effort to keep any program on the books that can be called COHORT. The current candidate program, the Package Replacement System, bears faint resemblance to the policies necessary to achieve cohesive units. This latest set of policies accedes almost entirely to the dictates of the individual replacement system. The main feature is replacements for combat units by tailored packages of small groups of replacements. The deficiencies are enormous. These groups are not integral small combat units or crews. They will not include small-unit leaders, sergeants, or lieutenants. They are designed to be traveling groups that, once at their destination, will not necessarily be kept together. In fact virtually every small-unit leader interviewed said he would break up such replacement packages and use them as individual replacements.[22]

Unless rescued by the chief of staff, this latest iteration of COHORT is an indication that this program will soon join many other worthwhile programs that are proposed, fail to become institutionalized, and are now just memories of former top-level Army leaders and their action officers who at the time had no higher priority.

The desire to create cohesive units within the U.S. Army has a long history. The most recent efforts were a direct result of the traumatic impact Vietnam had on the U.S. Army. As early as the early 1970s junior officers returning from Vietnam with lessons learned began questioning many policies that contributed to the unraveling of the U.S. Army in Vietnam. A major lesson relearned during Vietnam was that cohesive units perform better in combat and are also more able to withstand the stress of combat. So stark were these lessons that through correspondence and meetings between more junior officers and top Army leaders, such as the commander of the Military Personnel Center in 1974,[23] these issues began to bubble up within the Army, culminating in a decision by the chief of staff of the Army in 1979, General Edward Meyer, to formally set out the problem and solution through a Task Force on Army Cohesion and Stability (ARCOST).

By 1980 resolve within the Army to create cohesive units was at its high point. One year earlier at an inter-university seminar on armed forces and society attended by top Army leaders, the late Morris Janowitz, foremost American military sociologist of his time, stated that armies have known for hundreds of years how to create highly effective cohesive units. His question was: "Why doesn't the American Army want cohesive units?" General Meyer resolved to implement policies that would create cohesive units.

By 1988 it was clear to those who dared to look closely at the situation that this effort, begun in 1979–1980 with so much resolve by top Army leaders, was close to failure. The question "Why doesn't the American Army want cohesive units?" still remains. Perhaps it should be rephrased as: "Why can't the American Army create cohesive units?" This is a significant question. It has been suggested that we shouldn't worry too much about the lack of cohesion in peacetime because it will appear rapidly once war breaks out. Such responses indicate a lack of knowledge about unit cohesion, and the time and effort required to create high-performing cohesive units. To quote long-time researchers of cohesion, "It is a great American myth that cohesion will occur the moment we go into battle."[24]

The inability of top Army leaders to bring fundamental and lasting change to the Army through this program and others raises questions as to their basic understanding of the structure, functions, and patterns of behavior and process that shape the U.S. Army. In this case, basic errors in judgment appear to have been made in the decision to implement COHORT through an evolutionary process lasting years. As leaders and action officers changed, other priorities arose and the system was able to shrug off, attenuate, or just ignore the incremental policy changes intended to institutionalize cohesive units. Perhaps the greatest failure was the failure to create a constituency (e.g., division and unit commanders) within the Army that had a primary vested interest in the institutionalization of COHORT and related policies designed to create cohesive units. To leave the implementation in the hands of a DCSPER and Personnel Command community whose vested and substantial bias was and remains in favor of an individual replacement system deeply rooted in the current overall personnel system appears to have been a fundamental error.

In addition to the unabated turbulence discussed in a prior chapter and the irresolute implementation of a deeply flawed COHORT program that did not efficiently promote cohesion, other basic policies governing the selection and career management of small-unit leaders have become major factors working against the Army's ability to create and train high-performing units.

NOTES

1. It should be noted that many commanders in today's Army are very reluctant to acknowledge the possibility of such cohesion measurements, much less enthusiastically promote them, because they often indicate significant leadership lapses. As with any conservative organization, the Army is slow to move toward such measures even though they are valid assessments and point the way toward improvement in unit performance and warfighting capability.

2. See for example: D. H. Marlow et al., "Unit Manning System Evaluation," Technical Reports Nos. 1 through 5 (Washington, D.C.: Walter Reed Army Institute of Research (WRAIR) and the Army Research Institute (ARI) Values Survey briefing for the Army Committee for leadership and Values (Alexandria, Va., May 20, 1986).

3. All of these data are unclassified and have been made available to various elements of the Army's leadership.

4. For example, examine the histories of French Army units in North Africa in the late 1950s and early 1960, and the history of North Vietnam and Vietcong units from 1965 to 1970.

5. Charles C. Moskos and Frank R. Woods, eds., *The Military — More Than Just a Job?* (New York: Pergamon-Brassey's, 1988).

6. Review figures in this chapter. The phenomenon of the erosion of core soldier values is sometimes explained away as an unavoidable and natural trend that occurs the longer the soldier is in the Army. However, experience in other armies (e.g., NVA, IDF, French) belies this "natural" trend explanation.

7. Guy L. Siebold, "Army Values: Results of Theme Year Research," (Alexandria, Va.: ARI, January 1987), 2.

8. Robert Holz, Informal Briefing Chart (Alexandria, Va.: ARI, January 1988).

9. D. H. Marlow et al., "Unit Manning System Field Evaluation Technical Report No. 5." (Washington, D.C.: Walter Reed Army Institute of Research, June 1987).

10. Ibid., 1.

11. It should be noted that even at their highest measures, the highest scores were only slightly above the scale midpoint and could indicate cohesion was only slightly above average at its best.

12. Marlow et al., "Field Evaluation," 12–13.

13. See definition of cohesion in William D. Henderson, *Cohesion: The Human Element in Combat* (Washington, D.C.: National Defense University Press, 1985), 4.

14. Marlow et al., "Field Evaluation," 14.

15. Ibid., 15.

16. Ibid., 1, 7.

17. Siebold, "Army Values," 2.

18. Marlow et al., "Field Evaluation," 2.

19. K. R. Smith, "Dimensions of Morale" (Armidale NSW, Australia: Armidale College, 1987), 2.

20. While the COHORT program has failed to obtain its original objectives, its public relations efforts remain strong and even in early 1990 the public is generally unaware of its failure.

21. DCSPER, July 1987. The current Army posture on COHORT is to sustain by 1992 approximately 3 percent of the Army's combat companies as COHORT and sustain an additional 4 percent of non-COHORT companies through a package replacement system.

22. Unit Manning System, Information Update (Washington, D.C.: Office of the Deputy Chief of Staff for Personnel, February 1987), Number 1–87, 3.

23. See, W. D. Henderson, *Why the Viet Cong Fought: A Study of Motivation and Control in a Modern Army in Combat* (Westport, Conn.: Greenwood Press, 1979) and excerpt letter written in 1974 to M. G. Gard, MILPERCEN Commander.

24. Discussion among David Marlowe, Owen Jacobs, and the author at Army Research Institute, Alexandria, Va., 1987.

8

THE BROKEN BACKBONE

The negative impact of the Enlisted Personnel Management System (EPMS) on the NCO Corps since the early 1970s has been profound, but generally unrecognized or at least unacknowledged publicly. The U.S. Army Noncommissioned Officer Corps used to be referred to as "the backbone of the Army"; no more — the backbone is broken. Much of the cause for this change in the nature of the NCO Corps can be attributed to EPMS because EPMS has effected a subtle yet profound change in the basic function served by the NCO Corps for the U.S. Army.

Some of the policies and process through which the NCO Corps is currently managed (EPMS) and their deleterious effects on Army warfighting capability are:

- The three functions of an NCO Corps in any top professional army are generally: to train soldiers, to lead soldiers in small units in war, and to provide specialized technical expertise.
- Through the creation of a huge centralized bureaucracy to perform many functions not previously performed or previously performed at unit level, the U.S. Army has created a fourth but ill-defined NCO functional area: that of junior staff officer.
- The force structure supporting this fourth functional area has mushroomed with overall strength assigned to this centralized function now greater than the combined soldier and NCO strength for the three major combat arms: infantry, artillery, and armor.
- A significant portion of the quality NCO force structure is now dedicated to this fourth functional area. Only 17 percent of NCO strength, generally of low quality, is now dedicated toward combat units.

- The fourth functional area is absorbing enormous amounts of resources. For example, the administrative career field now has more sergeants major than any other field including infantry. Large numbers of top-quality NCOs are being absorbed by this functional area at the expense of the combat arms and warfighting capability (e.g., MOS 71 series [admin] has over 5,100 top-quality E-5–E-7 NCOs while the 19K series for armor struggles to make do with only 2,400 top-quality E-5–E-7 NCOs).
- Value added by the centralized management process is difficult to demonstrate. On the other hand, many contend that the fragmentation and centralization of manpower and personnel functions at Department of the Army level detract significantly from the commander's ability to form and maintain high-performing units.
- The net effect of the current EPMS on the NCO Corps has been to place the traditional NCO function of leading small units in combat as the bottom priority. Individualized and centralized career management of NCOs has led the great majority of NCOs away from long-term service with soldiers in small units.
- The NCO Corps no longer has as its primary function the training for and leading of soldiers in combat. The tremendous warfighting potential of the NCO Corps is being dissipated in ill-defined jobs, largely extraneous to warfighting. The NCO Corps will be a "broken backbone" until it returns to soldiers and units as its top priority.

The single most important functional purpose of an NCO Corps in any first-rate Army is effectively to join that Army's warriors, the soldiers and their needs, to the rest of the Army; its officers, weapons, goals, objectives, and the people and values it will defend. The joining of small-unit combat leaders, who are primarily NCOs, with the fighting soldiers of a nation is where the most effective and primarily leadership role takes place in an army. It is at this organizational level, where formal organization meets individual soldier, that the individual must be led into exposing himself to the stress and dangers of combat. Strong leadership is necessary if the soldier is to become part of a truly professional high-performing combat unit. The training and small-unit leader functions are the true callings of the NCO Corps. The technical function sometimes performed by NCOs is a more distant support function. The emergence of a fourth NCO function in the U.S. Army, that of junior staff officer, is having negative and unanticipated effects on the traditional NCO functions.

The first function of small-unit trainer/leader is not being performed well in the U.S. Army. The failure to achieve strong vertical bonding between soldiers and their sergeants, the continuing effects of unabated personnel turbulence, and the lack of quality NCOs in combat units described in earlier chapters explain the failure to achieve high marks in the training and leadership functions and can be followed back to the effects of EPMS.

Perhaps the most noticeable effect of EPMS has been the great expansion of NCO spaces since the early 1970s (see Figure 8.1) into many nontraditional areas so that many additional avenues for promotion and advancement are now possible beyond the traditional trainer/leader and technical routes. Currently, of the Army's approximately 280,000 NCOs, only about 17 percent are presently in the combat branches. Since 1980 NCO ranks have grown at three times the rate of the overall enlisted force. Today NCOs comprise almost 40 percent of the Army's active force.[1] Over 80 percent of the Army's NCOs now fill technical or administrative jobs, which in many cases are similar to junior staff jobs with ill-defined functional duties not well related to warfighting.

One method for making sense of the effects EPMS is having on the NCO Corps is through structural-functional analysis. This sounds like a formidable undertaking but in reality it can be a straightforward and relatively simple analytical method that produces useful assessments.[2] In the areas of manpower, personnel, and training (MPT) this approach simply asks what functions must be performed by NCOs if the Army is to endure and be successful in its basic mission. The matching of structure (e.g., NCO Corps) to function (e.g., small-unit leader) within a specific context or environment can then serve as the basis to assess the overall process of organizations performing functions resulting in actions that either promote the purpose of the Army or that lessen or hinder the ability of the organization to survive in its environment or in the case of the Army an anticipated environment (i.e., war).

Chapter 1 discussed the fragmentation of responsibility for various MPT functions among a wide number of organizations scattered throughout the Army but under the centralized control of the Army staff. Along with the fragmentation of responsibility for such functions as training and personnel selection and assignment has been the enormous expansion of agencies and organizations over the past fifteen years such as field operating agencies (FOAs) that require enormous amounts of dollars and people to perform their small part of these overall functions. As indicated previously, this expansion of centralized organizations has been one of the major reasons for the great increase in the number of

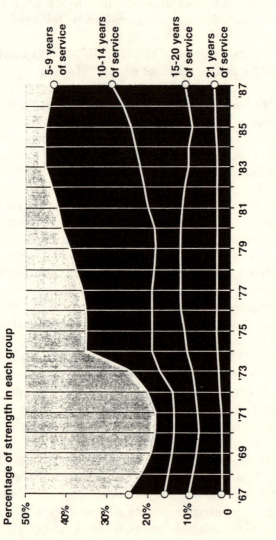

Percentage of strength in each group

5-9 years of service

10-14 years of service

15-20 years of service

21 years of service

50% 40% 30% 20% 10% 0

'67 '69 '71 '73 '75 '77 '79 '81 '83 '85 '87

FIGURE 8.1 — Rise in NCOs since Vietnam War (*Source: Army Times* 8/8/88)

officers and NCOs in the Army force structure. Unfortunately, instead of preparing the Army to fight wars more efficiently it is becoming apparent that the personnel in many of these organizations would contribute little to warfighting in the event of war. Contribution to warfighting can be simply defined as any significant output or product of an organization that contributes directly and substantively within the first thirty to sixty days of war to the performance of a combat unit with a wartime mission. Keeping in mind Soviet strategic reliance on surprise and speed of attack and the possibility of other Third World conflicts such as occurred in Grenada and the Falklands, the winning or losing of a war in thirty plus days is not unrealistic.

In this regard the U.S. Army is paying a tremendous price for a centralized MPT process that contributes little to combat power and warfighting capability. A portion of this price is the enormous expense involved in the large number of NCOs assigned to centralized organizations with functional responsibilities that are not clearly defined and of doubtful contribution to warfighting. The large and unproductive personnel float required by the individual replacement system and its inherent turbulence combined with the expanded numbers of active Army and civilian positions made necessary by the fragmentation and centralization of functions (e.g., personnel assignments, promotions, professional development, data processing, message traffic, etc.) at Department of Army level requires that a conservatively estimated one-third of active Army strength (soldier and civilian) be continuously sacrificed to a process that contributes little to warfighting capability.

The effects of this inefficient process on the NCO Corps have been significant. Only 17 percent of the NCO Corps now serve with combat units, and these assignments, as evidenced by promotion rates, are not seen as primary routes to successful careers as NCOs. While an increase in NCO positions can be demonstrated in almost all military occupational specialties (MOS), some have grown enormously in order to serve centralized functions at the expense of the combat arms. For example, the combined total of soldiers and NCOs serving in active infantry, field artillery, and armor combat units at any one time is significantly less than the number of soldiers and NCOs serving in administration (MOS 71), signal (MOS 31), and supply (MOS 76), which totals over 138,000. When combined with tens of thousands of civilians also serving in these last three service areas, the overall number becomes ridiculously high. There are more signalmen (radio operators, etc.) assigned to the U.S. Army in Europe than there are infantrymen. In the continental United States (CONUS) the numbers are just as questionable. The continuous creation of new headquarters, offices, directorates, FOAs, and other agencies to execute the centralization of many functions previously performed at unit levels has required enormous additional manpower. For example, where until several years ago there was no requirement for it, one organization, the expanded Enlisted Soldier Evaluation Center, now processes over 550,000 documents a month. These communications are put on microfiche, screened, and evaluated. As discussed later in the chapter, the value added by this organization is doubtful.

It is likely that this overall process is detrimental to the commander's ability to create and maintain high-performing units. However, the main point here is that enormous dollars and personnel costs are involved in operating this process. For example, the administrative career field (CMF 71) now has a population of over 51,000 soldiers and many additional civilians in related jobs for a total personnel administrative force of about 70,000. Administrative soldier strength of over 51,000 includes over 540 sergeants major positions, the highest number of any career management field. This is more than the infantry, the field artillery, or the armor CMFs. It is also notable that over 40 percent of the admin CMF is comprised of NCO positions. This includes thousands of top-quality (top one-third AFQT) NCOs. Specifically, there are over 5,100 top-quality NCOs (E-5–E-7) assigned to CMF 71. When compared to the sparse total of about 2,400 (E-5–E-7) top-quality NCOs assigned to the armor CMF (MOS 19K, Abrams tank, and 19E, M60 tank), the cost to the warfighting function imposed by the current centralized system becomes apparent.

The nature of the function performed by these centralized organizations should be questioned. The value added by their participation should be weighed against the dollars and manpower they require to perform their function. The ever-increasing centralization of manpower and personnel functions, in addition to being enormously expensive, is also dysfunctional, in that it hinders the commander in the field in his pursuit of cohesive highly effective units.

Perhaps the most pernicious effect of EPMS results from its centralized management of all the actions and decisions viewed as most important in an NCO's career such as promotions, assignments, and professional schooling. As a result, NCOs have come to view their commanders and their unit as of secondary importance in influencing these vital decisions. Rather they look to an artificial, centralized and distant administrative process located in Washington, D.C., as the source of career advancement. A revealing insight into the nature of the Army's centralized personnel system and its direct relationship with the individual soldier and NCO is presented in a front-page story of the July 25, 1988, edition of the *Army Times,* entitled "How to Tame TAPA: An Enlisted Man's Guide to the Army's Personnel Bureaucracy." This article makes clear the dominant and direct role the centralized bureaucracy has over the soldier's career at the expense of the local commander and unit. For example, dictates from the central system such as promotions out of the job/unit or professional development requirements almost always take precedence over unit needs and priorities. The criteria used as the basis for administering this centralized system are similar to those used in administering the Officer's Personnel Management System. Thus recent observations by some in the Army's top leadership that NCOs are beginning to act like officers in pursuing ticket punching and other "careerist" behavior should not be surprising. EPMS rewards this type of behavior.

Illustrative of the great detail assumed by the Total Army Personnel Command (formerly TAPA) for managing NCO careers through EPMS are the following excerpts from the centralized assignment procedure of "CAP III" in its former version.[3] Through centralized review of NCO records, "CAP III special instructions will show the career development needs of each NCO" and will provide two specific assignment options for each NCO's military occupational specialty for all types of units. NCOs are cautioned that they should ensure that their personnel records maintained in Washington, D.C. are accurate and up to date and they should have "enlisted preference statements reflecting their assignment wishes on file at MILPERCEN."

No other army in the world assumes this level of centralized micromanagement for its soldiers. In fact other armies have examined the U.S. system and rejected it as not only cost ineffective but also for bypassing the local commander and seriously hindering the maintenance of cohesion and high-performing units.

The basic thinking behind EPMS was that the Officer Personnel Management System (OPMS) initiated by the Army earlier appeared to be successful for managing officers and therefore should be a suitable model for managing noncommissioned officers as well. The blind assumption that centralized personnel practices appropriate for managing officers must also be good for managing NCOs is unsupported. Officers serve widely different organizational functions than NCOs. Certainly no comparative structural-functional analyses were made that compared the different roles, missions, and tasks of officers with those of NCOs and then asked if similar centralized management systems and policies were appropriate for both officers and NCOs.

Instead, after the decision to implement EPMS, widespread actions ensued by the various Army proponents of various career management fields to put in place attractive career paths that promised each CMF its share of top promotions and desired locations throughout the Army. This process was in part based on a process that perceived "inequities in promotion opportunities between career fields" that caused other proponents to increase "senior authorizations to enhance promotion opportunity," which "contributed to over documentation" supporting NCO spaces and caused "other proponents to request senior grade increases."[4] In other words, much of the recent growth in the NCO Corps had little to do with increasing the Army's warfighting capability.

What has emerged is that over two-thirds of the senior NCO (E-8 and E-9) positions, and 83 percent or approximately 230,000 of current E-5 through E-7 NCO ranks, can now be achieved without pursuing the traditional route to the top through the combat arms. By 1988 the career field with the most top NCO positions, that of sergeant major, was not in the combat arms but was in the administrative field, which is now authorized 542 sergeants major.

The many additional avenues for promotion and the centralized priority placed by the Department of the Army on many noncombat fields, reinforced by high promotion rates for these jobs, have attracted most of the Army's quality NCOs toward these fields. As noted earlier very few of the Army's 82,500 top-quality NCOs are in the combat arms. This attraction away from units is reinforced by promotion rates. Many NCOs assigned to noncombat unit assignments enjoy very high promotion rates (e.g., 97 percent for USAREC from E-6 to E-7) while the corresponding average promotion rate for NCOs assigned to combat units is approximately 10 percent, the lowest of the four functional NCO areas.

The institutional attraction away from the combat jobs has been very strong. In addition to higher promotion rates and choice assignments, the relative comfort and easier life associated with administrative and staff duties over the more strenuous, uncomfortable, and dangerous field duties associated with the combat arms must attract many NCOs, especially when reinforced by the higher priority the Army appears to give these jobs.

A basic and underlying reason for the high priority enjoyed by the NCO junior staff functional area is the lack of any definitive Army policy outlining which NCO functions are most important and therefore which should receive priority in assignments, grade structure, promotion, quality, and so on. Presumably the combined trainer/small-unit leader function (warfighting) should receive priority. This is not the case. The basic assumption governing the priorities affecting NCO functions and manifest in decisions about distribution of numbers and quality is the assumption of bureaucratic equity. The operation of this basic ground rule becomes apparent when the allocation of promotions and grade structure are under review. For example, this becomes very apparent when the Army personnel community holds periodic general officer personnel proponents meetings. This meeting is attended by the generals or their deputies representing the various Army branches. Invariably, personnel distribution issues come up for resolution. For example, the chief of chaplains will present data and state that he is not receiving his full share of quality soldiers or bring up another similar distributional issue. The ensuing discussion generally evolves toward all branches getting their "fair share." No one questions this assumption of bureaucratic equity and no one raises the issue of the necessity for clear policies reflecting priority for small-unit leaders in NCO quality, grade structure, and assignments.

Given the lack of an Army policy with real teeth (grade struc- ture, promotions, quality, etc.) directing NCO Corps priorities to- ward warfighting functions, NCOs are left to migrate at will among the four NCO functions in pursuit of their individual careers. As noted earlier, the higher promotion rates, better assignments, and easier garrison life associated with the junior staff and technical functions seriously detract from the trainer/small-unit leader func- tions with their more difficult duties, less desirable assignments, and lower promotion rates. Examples of career attractions away from the NCO trainer/combat function are plentiful. Typical is the follow- ing article from *Pentagram* which in one respect is a help wanted ad without any regard for what Army priorities should be for NCOs.:

Are you an outstanding private first class or specialist four . . . who wants to get promoted faster? Then consider training and duty in MOS 71, Executive Administrative Assistant.

According to . . . the Director of Personnel . . . at the Adjutant General School . . . soldiers in this MOS provide senior officers with indispensable administrative support. They prepare correspondence and screen telephone calls and office visitors for their supervisors. . . .

The promotion opportunities to SP4 and Sgt. are excellent in MOS 71C. In fiscal year 1986, all eligible SP4s received promotion to Sgt.

If you meet the course prerequisites . . . you should volunteer for training in this MOS.[5]

The NCO Corps began to depart from its basic functions of trainer and small-unit leader in the early 1970s and began to emphasize junior staff functions. A basic cause was the need for the Army to adapt to an unsympathetic domestic environment that emerged in the 1970s as a result of the Vietnam War. The volunteer Army emerged and with it basic changes in the structure and function of the NCO Corps. By the early 1980s it was apparent that the NCO Corps was beginning to lose its way. Parts of an article I wrote in 1982 are almost identical to portions of the chief of staff's 1987 Leader Development Study on NCO leadership. In 1982 the causes of change and their effects on the NCO Corps were already apparent. More specifically:

> The impetus for these changes came from a variety of sources: Congress, the Court of Military Appeals and even internally as the Army made major changes in policy in attempts to preempt further criticism. A very significant effect of such policy changes was a pronounced shift in authority away from squad leaders, platoon sergeants, first sergeants and company commanders.
>
> Higher commanders tightened up on discretionary authority delegated to these subordinate leaders as they centralized authority in an attempt to decrease the possibility of future "embarrassing incidents." Senior staffs also became very "risk-conscious": they advised their commanders, with the Judge Advocate General and the Public Affairs Office leading the wave of safe-sided advice with little or no thought given to its effect on unit cohesion.
>
> While they were protecting the commander, they were also making his job of building cohesive, combat-ready units enormously difficult.
>
> In effect, NCOs became bystanders as higher ranks reduced their authority and discontinued many of their traditional responsibilities and functions. As the FORSCOM commander (at the time) said, "NCOs are not fully utilized while commanders and other senior officers are working as hard as they can" . . . this situation has evolved because of a serious imbalance between NCO responsibilities on one hand and NCO authority on the other.
>
> There has been much discussion in recent years about allowing NCOs to do their jobs by returning their responsibility for training soldiers. . . .
>
> Unfortunately, while much responsibility has been pushed in the direction of NCOs, little real authority has accompanied it. Company, battalion, and brigade commanders and their staffs are never far off and are always prepared to interject themselves into NCO business through frequent forays under the principle of "management by exception."
>
> Faced with this significant loss of authority over the past 15 years, the intrinsic nature of the NCO Corps is changing. Fewer and fewer squad leaders and platoon sergeants, once referred to as the "backbone of the Army" now exist — those who knew their jobs better than any others, who loved their troops and expected to be with them indefinitely unless they got lucky and made company first sergeant.
>
> Large segments of NCOs are turning away from the traditional path leading to a successful career: squad leader, platoon sergeant, first sergeant.[6]

Such was one view of the NCO Corps in 1982. Unfortunately, the situation appears to persist today. As noted in the August 1987 version of the leader development study, "there is much confusion about the role of the NCO and his duties, about his responsibilities and his authority."[7] Large segments of the NCO Corps have turned away from the traditional and clear path leading to a successful career: team leader, squad leader, platoon sergeant, and perhaps first sergeant. Instead, the NCO presently finds himself increasingly in ill-defined functional roles with duties often resembling those of a junior staff officer and, according to the leader development study, with "little delegation of authority or assignment of additional authority . . . consequently NCOs too often do not exercise initiative and instead want to be told what to do."[8]

The recent article by John C. Bahnsen and James W. Bradin, "The Army's Command Sergeant Major Problem," is a look at these same problems focusing on the position of command sergeant major.[9] The authors recognize the need to link the top NCO rank to the rest of the NCO Corps. They maintain there should be no command sergeants major (CSM) positions away from troop units. "There is no damn need for a CSM above brigade level . . . there are damn few greater responsibilities than taking care of soldiers and preparing them for battle, and our newly exalted CSMs don't do these things."

Although Bahnsen and Bradin don't relate their views on the CSM position directly to EPMS, their message is very similar to the theme of this chapter that the trainer/leader function of the NCO Corps is primary. They state: "The Army needs the skills and talents of its superb noncommissioned officer corps down with the troops. It's essential that we have them teaching and training our young soldiers. There is no calling more important."[10]

It can be argued that a centralized management system is necessary for officers, especially for majors and above, because of the widely varying functions and roles that officers play throughout the Army. It is much more difficult to make the same argument for NCOs. The three primary and defensible roles of the NCO Corps, those of trainer, unit troop leader, and technician, have been historically performed best when management of these functions has been decentralized.[11]

Perhaps a more effective way of describing the major shortcoming of the centralized EPMS system is to say that it focuses on the individual rather than on the unit and what that unit requires to become a first-rate combat unit. Soldiers don't fight most effectively as individuals but as members of a unit with strong leaders who have achieved the trust and confidence of their soldiers.[12] Occasionally, the Army is still able to produce first-rate squads and platoons. When it does, however, it is because of outstanding small-unit leaders. The requisites of small-unit leadership for high unit performance were made clear in a recent report by Colonel (ret.) Mike Malone. His description of unit performance and the NCO leadership involved was exciting. The NCOs involved were clearly committed to the unit trainer/leader function.[13] Unfortunately, this level of performance does not appear to be the norm. To ensure the development of this type of unit and leadership, NCOs must view their unit as the primary source of career advancement in such vital areas as promotions, assignments, and professional schooling.

There are many indicators that most NCOs do not presently view such assignments as a primary track to career advancement. The low promotion rates and low quality associated with assignments to combat units have already been examined. These data are supported by an Army-wide survey that showed that almost half of the NCOs surveyed did not want to be assigned to COHORT units because of the perception that the length of the assignment would interfere with the development of their careers.[14] What is even more noteworthy was the lack of interest in such data by members of the Army's personnel community. Normally, it should be expected that troop-leading assignments in combat units should be a much-sought-after and professionally rewarding path to advancement. Not so under EPMS. The data and professional experiences of the past fifteen years indicate to the NCO Corps that promotions and desirable assignments are much easier to come by away from combat units. The recent study on NCO professional development indicates that 75 percent of the NCO Corps felt NCO promotions should be linked to attendance at NCO schools.[15] No mention was made of performance in the unit. Further, 63 percent stated that the EPMS process is helping their careers and 83 percent said they were pleased with their career progress under EPMS. Again, there was no mention of duty performance in the unit as a basis for measuring career progress nor did the study ask any questions that reflected on the unit.

This lack of emphasis on the unit was brought home clearly to the Army when it began to fill the small unit NCO spaces recently required by the Army's new light divisions. Contrary to what one would expect, the U.S. Army did not have its quality NCOs pressing for assignment to positions recognized by top armies throughout the world as essential to be filled by the best leaders available. Instead the U.S. Army was forced to "dragoon" NCOs, many of whom were "marginally qualified and resentful" of being assigned a new division after having made other "career plans."[16] As might have been expected, the leadership provided by many NCOs did not result in the trust and confidence necessary to link and bond the soldiers in these units with the goals and core professional values of the units. The great turbulence among many of the NCOs initially assigned and then relieved, transferred, or eliminated made it very difficult for the soldiers to identify with their leaders or their unit: "Sergeant X is our fourth squad leader. Just when we get to know our sergeant he gets chaptered or busted or falls apart physically."[17]

The question remains: Why can't an Army with almost 300,000 NCOs assigned, many of whom are of the highest quality, and supported by a training system that is more sophisticated than that of any other Army, produce the requisite quality small-unit leaders? The short answer is that EPMS does not serve the unit and meet the requirements necessary to produce top-performing cohesive units. Rather EPMS serves the individual through a remote centralized system that takes from the unit and local commander the prerogatives necessary to control those aspects of the unit vital to creating high-performing units. For example, Figures 8.2 and 8.3 outline the current centralized EPMS approach to the acquisition, classification, assignment, training deployment, sustainment, promotion, and development of soldiers and NCOs. The great emphasis on COHORT over the past eight years notwithstanding, the obvious focus on the individual system at the expense of the needs of the unit and the local commander to produce and sustain high-performing units is overwhelming.

Figure 8.2 shows the mission of the centralized Enlisted Personnel Management Division (EPMD) and explains why the emphasis on managing the individual persists in spite of the COHORT program. Certainly, if the mission of EPMD were decentralized and changed to support local commanders and efforts to create high-performing cohesive units, by providing stable units and long-term top quality small-unit leadership, the mission statement would read much differently.

Figure 8.3 with nearly 400 individual Military Occupational Specialties (MOSs) shows the real drivers behind the nature of EPMS and why it is presently managed on an individual basis. Simply put, if the factors depicted in this figure reflect the priorities of the personnel management system as the mission chart of EPMD suggests they do, then the organizational requisites necessary for building and sustaining high-performing cohesive combat units will never be present. A personnel management system with a total possible 473,850 individual-type positions to be kept filled by a centralized management division guided by a management philosophy that constantly keeps the entire system in motion will be indefinitely chasing its tail. It will never produce in

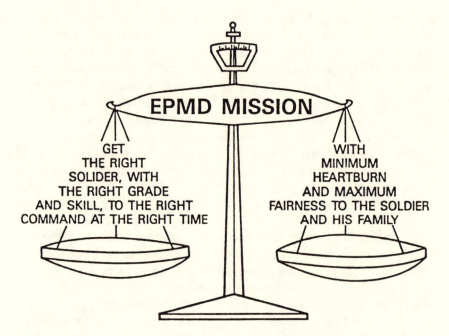

FIGURE 8.2 — EPMD Mission (*Source:* U.S. Army Military Personnel Center, Enlisted Personnel Management Division, Washington, D.C.)

sufficient numbers quality units capable of matching the combat power of similar units in other armies.

The policies and procedures that govern the personnel management system outlined in Figures 8.2 and 8.3 are for the most part contained in Army Regulations 614-200, 614-30, and 614-5, covering enlisted personnel assignments, training, overseas duty, tour stabilization, and changes of duty assignments. An overview reveals an extremely complex system that is fragmented in its execution with inconsistencies abounding and managed with great difficulty. The turbulence, quality control, and promotion problems discussed previously are merely representative of the system problems to be faced. The amount of routine communications message traffic required to keep this centralized system going is enormous and not necessary under a decentralized system. Even after years of effort, data automation is still not satisfactory or even fully available to implement policy and monitor the system. Certainly, the complexity of the system would become overwhelming given the overload data requirements of mobilization.

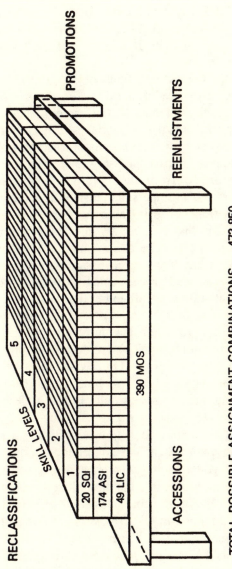

RECLASSIFICATIONS

SKILL LEVELS

1 2 3 4 5

20 SQI
174 ASI
49 LIC

390 MOS

PROMOTIONS

REENLISTMENTS

ACCESSIONS

TOTAL POSSIBLE ASSIGNMENT COMBINATIONS   473,850
FY 85 MTOE/TDA CHANGES   3.7 MILLION

FIGURE 8.3 — Force Alignment Program (*Source*: U.S. Army Military Personnel Center, Accession, Training and Retention Management Division, Washington, D.C.)

The experience with the COHORT program demonstrates the inability of centralized EPMS to adapt. As the COHORT program expanded, even minimally, it became apparent to the system managers at MILPERCEN and unit personnel officers throughout the Army that centralized EPMS could not support COHORT and that extensive off-line management efforts were required to make the program work. Eventually this became a major factor in the demise of COHORT in spite of the desire of many top Army leaders to see it succeed.

The subtle but potentially disastrous faults of EPMS are illustrated by looking at the effects of centralized promotions for NCOs. Probably no other single event is as significant in an NCO's career than a promotion. Promotions recognizing service to the unit and the Army are probably the unit commanders strongest positive tool in reinforcing outstanding performance and building the norms necessary to create cohesive units. To have this tool removed from the commander's control and administered instead through an impersonal, distant bureaucracy on the basis of seemingly artificial criteria removed from the day-to-day performance of the NCO in his unit strongly inhibits the commander's ability to build cohesive units. The commander no longer has the authority to promote NCOs based on a direct relationship to performance in the unit. Instead, a centralized process using artificial cut-off scores based on superficial evaluations of inflated enlisted efficiency reports (EERs), a 5" x 7" glossy photograph, and reports on schools attended is used to determine who gets promoted. The unit commander is left only with the negative option of pulling an NCO's name off of a promotion list or from consideration for promotion. Otherwise, the commander's influence is limited to the degree he desires to inflate an EER in order to get it noticed among thousands of other similar EERs. In describing the current NCO promotion system and its strong tendency toward inflation and inability to allow "field commanders to clearly distinguish between average soldiers and those who . . . achieve excellence," one member of the Army staff said: "It's gotten to the point where nearly everybody on a selection list gets 200 point scores [the maximum] from his commander and unit board."[18] The appalling process as used by a current NCO promotion board was explained in all seriousness in a recent *Soldiers* magazine article appropriately entitled "Paper Chase."[19]

In spite of an advanced automated management information system that supports EPMS, the article explained that MILPERCEN's enlisted records and evaluation center receives more than 550,000 documents each month, among them the EERs and photographs needed to conduct a recent E-7 promotion board. The Board Interface Branch at

MILPERCEN was required to handle over 1 million pieces of paper to support the E-7 board deliberations. This is mind boggling considering the man hours, facilities, and other resources now required to perform a function that was previously and more efficiently performed in the field on the back of an envelope.

Judged on its ability to produce high-performing cohesive fighting units, EPMS is a failure. Even judged on its own terms it fails because of its complexity and its failure to meet the problems of personnel turbulence, the need for quality leaders in combat units, and policies that seriously hinder the commander's ability to produce cohesion. The U.S. Army today is paying a huge price for a system that at best is often irrelevant to warfighting ability and one that at worst limits in many respects the combat power of the U.S. Army.

Until the EPMS is restructured to focus NCO career priorities on continuous service in troop units in support of the trainer/leader function, the backbone of the Army will remain broken and the U.S. Army will not achieve the stable, long-term, quality small-unit leadership necessary to build the high-performing and cohesive combat units necessary to win on today's battlefields.

NOTES

1. "Growth of NCO Ranks Outstrips Total Enlisted in Recent Years," *Army Times*, February 8, 1988, 4, 24.

2. See, for example, Robert K. Merton, *Social Theory and Social Structure: Toward the Codification of Theory and Research*, rev. ed. (Glencoe, Ill.: Free Press, 1957), or Marion J. Levy, *The Structure of Society* (Princeton, N.J.: Princeton University Press, 1952).

3. *Pentagram*, December 4, 1986, 3.

4. "Senior Enlisted Grade Restructure," DCSPER Briefing, 1986.

5. *Pentagram*, February 5, 1987, 9.

6. William Darryl Henderson, "Can-Do NCOs — With Clout — Can Help Cohesion Problems," *Army*, March 1982, 18–22.

7. "Leader Development Study" (Fort Leavenworth, Kans.: Combined Arms Center, 1987), 22.

8. Ibid., 23.

9. John C. Bahnsen and James W. Bradin, "The Army's Command Sergeant Major Problem," *Parameters*, June 1988, 9–17.

10. Ibid., 12.

11. Peter W. Kuzumplich, summary of manuscript on *Comparative Wartime Replacement Systems* (Washington, D.C.: Defense Intelligence Agency, November, 1986).

12. See, for example, the historical lesson of leadership cited by the well-known military historian Jay Luvass, who states in reference to the Battle of Gettysburg that

"the biggest lesson for company grade officers out of the battle was the trust and confidence of the men in their officers." *Pentagram,* November 23, 1986, 1.

13.   Dandridge M. Malone, "With the Mountain Men," ARI Report No. DAAL03-86-D-0001 (Alexandria, Va.: ARI, 1988).

14.   ARI, "U.S. Army Soldier Values Survey" (Alexandria, Va.: ARI, 1987).

15.   Sergeants' Business, "NCO Professional Development: A Report to the NCO Corps." Sponsored by The Office of the Chief of Public Affairs Headquarters, Department of the Army (Washington, D.C., February 1986).

16.   D. H. Marlowe et al., "Unit Manning System Field Evaluation Technical Report No. 5." (Washington, D.C.: Walter Reed Army Institute of Research, June 1987), 10.

17.   Ibid.

18.   Jim Tice, "Army May Revamp NCO Promotion Point Worksheet," *Army Times,* March 13, 1989, 3.

19.   "Paper Chase," *Soldiers* (July 1985): 69.

9

IT'S BROKE AND
NEEDS TO BE FIXED

A concluding one-sentence summation of the preceding eight chapters could read "The mediocre to average unit performance and the discouragingly low numbers of combat troops that characterize today's Army are a direct result of deeply rooted organizational inefficiencies that are apparent in the Army's manpower, personnel, and training (MPT) organization and policies."

Evidence presented in the preceding chapters in support of this conclusion contrasts sharply with recent statements by many top Army leaders that the Army has never been in better shape. The view that today's Army is the best ever defends the status quo by contrasting the quality and weapons of today's Army with those of the difficult post-Vietnam period — the era of the well-known "hollow Army." This view looks back to what was and says with some justification, "look how we have improved." A second view presented in the preceding chapters examines today's Army as it is and finds it seriously deficient. The potential enemy armies we would likely face in event of war have formidable human and technical capabilities. The U.S. Army looks good when compared internally to its recent past. However, in terms of absolute measures and its capability against potential enemy armies it is still only in the mediocre to average range in many key measures of warfighting capability.

This critical view has not been previously documented in such detail as it has been here and it is certainly not a view held widely in the U.S. Army, but it is supported privately by many, including our Allies. As one high-ranking member of Germany's Ministry of Defense, who shall remain anonymous, told me in reference to the continuing controversy about what the NATO allies spend on defense: "The U.S. should not look at the dollar amount the U.S. is spending on defense . . . look instead at what you are getting for your money. You spend over half your budget on people but much is wasted because you do not use them efficiently."

Evidence presented previously supports this view that much of the U.S. Army has turned into a sluggish, top-heavy bureaucracy with too many organizational layers and very long lines of support to soldiers in fighting units. This view sees mid- and upper-Army organization characterized by duplicative and extremely fragmented functional responsibilities that are the source of the recent and great growth in the numbers of NCOs and officers as well as headquarters, support agencies, information commands, and administrative organizations. Underlying this centralized organizational growth is a somewhat dated organizational ethos of "bigger is better." As a result this centralized bureaucracy absorbs enormous amounts of manpower (quality personnel) and dollars and is the major contributor to a severe case of the hardening of organizational arteries that increasingly resists the flow of needed support to the warfighting Army.

The history of U.S. involvement in war, especially in Europe, is one of an unwieldy system being initially overwhelmed by a fast-moving opponent's surprise and mass. Essential to eventual U.S. success has been time to reorganize and mobilize in order to bring to bear superior technology and materials. A comprehensive view of competing strategies from the viewpoint of potential enemies as well as from the U.S. viewpoint will indicate that the United States no longer has this advantage. Nevertheless, the U.S. Army has constructed a huge and unwieldy central bureaucracy tentatively aimed at long-term mobilization. Among the major armies of today's world, the U.S. Army alone relies upon a centralized manpower, personnel, and training organization to form and maintain its fighting units. The reasons for this are historically rooted in our mobilization for World War II. General George Marshall's vision of how to move most efficiently from an army of under 200,000 to one that would quickly total over 12 million was rooted in the then-modern phenomenon of Henry Ford's assembly line. The vision was to train men in specific skills represented by a number and then use them as interchangeable spare parts to man the enormous amounts of war equipment being produced by the United States. If your strategy is to overwhelm the enemy by the materials of war as the U.S. strategy in fact was during World War II, then the manpower challenge in support of that strategy became to supply enough men to man the equipment.

This is not, and cannot be, U.S. strategy today, and yet we remain saddled with a manpower, personnel, and training system that is deeply rooted in our mobilization experience of World War II. While it is capable of producing trained individual soldiers, it also has sharp limitations. Among the limitations of such a system are the following characteristics quoted from a perceptive historical review that focuses on the individual soldier rather than units:

1) Focused on mobilization rather than sustainment. . . .
2) Produced specialized soldiers as individual spare parts in assembly line process . . . while possibly appropriate for mobilization, elaborate classification made the system unresponsive during sustainment. The U.S. Army had some 802 district individual specialties . . . as opposed to the 20 found in a German armored division.
3) Unsuccessfully tried to provide individuals by grade and narrowly defined specialty through an intricate requisitioning process.
4) Produced too many specialists and a critical shortage of riflemen by November, 1944. Through late 1944, infantrymen were dregs of the Army rather than its elite.
5) Shipment of individuals as spare parts to be plugged into unit vacancies. Men were committed to combat within hours of joining strange units, before they had time to know or care about their comrades.
6) The emphasis on the individual was carried to the point that whole regiments were dissolved to provide individuals to fill shortages in committed units. More than anything else, it probably caused the low volume of fire noted by SLA Marshall and William DuPuy . . . judged in terms of unit cohesion, the American system was a failure. Ironically, it was equally a failure when judged by its own objectives because its very complexity made it impossible to maintain units at strength. American infantry companies routinely operated with strengths no greater than their foreign counterparts. *A huge price was paid for a goal that was irrelevant to combat power and couldn't be achieved anyway.*[1]

The nature of the MPT structure of today's Army is not very different from the historical structure described. In fact, the Army has attempted, unsuccessfully to date, to automate and perfect the centralized individual replacement system using computer technology. In the process it has created a proportionately larger and more costly centralized structure than ever before. In support of its enhanced centralized structure the Army, over the past fifteen years, has created in support of MPT functions numerous additional headquarters, field operating agencies, information commands, and administrative organizations. Much of this organization has been described previously. It is sufficient to emphasize here the enormous amounts of manpower and dollars consumed by this new centralized structure at the expense of warfighting units, and little value is added by these new organizations and the products they contribute to warfighting. As previously discussed, for example, the value added by the centralized promotion system for soldiers up to and including the rank of first sergeant (E-8) is extremely questionable. It can be demonstrated that the process is inefficient, costly, and actually has unintended effects that work against unit cohesion and performance. Certainly the commanders and senior NCOs at company and battalion levels know who is most deserving of promotion and who could best serve the unit if promoted. Promotions on this basis are traditional in all armies, and in wartime it is the only system that is practical as well as efficient. Instead the Army has diverted personnel spaces in the thousands costing hundreds of millions of dollars to produce a centralized administrative system that in the end is forced to make NCO promotions on the basis of inflated enlisted efficiency reports and 5" x 7" glossy photos. As explained in the preceding chapter, this process significantly weakens the unit by causing the soldier to look to a distant and impersonal centralized system to further his career rather than to his commander and unit. What becomes mind boggling is the consideration that this one small fragment of a function, that until recently was performed in the field as the duty of the commander, now requires significant manpower and money to record and evaluate over a half million routine documents centrally received every month. In addition, promotion boards often require over 1 million separate pieces of paper to be assembled in Washington, D.C., in support of board proceedings that in the end are forced to rely primarily on distorted and inflated efficiency reports and photographs, poor substitutes for the intimate knowledge available to the chain of command at unit level.

This inefficiency is repeated for hundreds of functions. Instead of limiting itself to the traditional functions of policy and inspection, the Army centralized structure has taken partial or complete operational responsibility for hundreds of similar functions. In an attempt to support the centralization of functions the personnel bureaucracy has created over 200 personnel information management systems, and yet routine inquiries are met by the response that current information regarding, for instance, soldier assignments and location are still six months out of date. Repeated failure is met with increased efforts at centralization. In 1984 the Army centralized all of its information management to include computer management, telecommunications, visual information records management, publishing, printing, libraries, and even mailrooms under a recently created central command, the Army Information Systems Command. With an annual budget approaching $3 billion and over 40,000 personnel assigned, these information managers join other major operators of the centralized structure such as the personnel administrators, the communicators, and the trainers. Each is given responsibility for a vertical portion of a fragmented function along with enormous manpower and dollar resources, yet the contribution of these communities to warfighting is, in many cases, doubtful. For example, the training function is fragmented. Commanders have responsibility for training their units yet the preponderance of training resources is given to Training and Doctrine Command (TRADOC). This command is given over 100,000 personnel, billions of dollars, and countless hours of soldiers' time each year and yet its mission is limited to training individual soldiers. The results of this fragmented approach for unit performance, as seen in Chapter 4, have been less than impressive. Another centralized functional area that has seemingly grown without constraint is Army communication. With no agreed doctrine of command and control such as broad mission orders or wide delegation of authority such as successfully employed in World War II, each of the Army's many headquarters puts a high priority on elaborate and redundant communications systems that allow communications among almost all possible levels of organization. With no workable theory of command and control, and responsibility divided through fragmented and duplicative functional areas, everyone with access to a radio or telephone feels obliged to participate in the never-ending powwow. As a result the signal branch is now one of the Army's largest. It is larger than both the armor and artillery branches and there are now more signal troops assigned to Europe than there are infantrymen. A workable theory of command and control for Army forces during wartime is urgently needed to constrain and stem the open-ended consumption of resources in support of increasingly centralized communications.

A strong suspicion exists among many observers of today's Army that an enormous price is being paid for a centralized process that produces products that are irrelevant to combat power and warfighting. Further, persistent centralization over the past fifteen years is seen as being based on the cost accounting assumption that bigger is better in terms of efficiency and performance, yet this has proven false worldwide. At a time when big business, governments, and even the Soviet Union and the U.S. Air Force are decentralizing under a "power-down" approach, the U.S. Army persists in trying to perfect the impossible.[2]

The Army urgently needs to assess its overall organizational structure in terms of the functions performed, the level at which they are performed, and especially the value added by each organizational element throughout the structure. It is recommended that a structural-functional method of analysis, as discussed in Chapter 8, be utilized as the basis for assessing each organization's contribution or hindrance to warfighting. An organizational contribution to warfighting is defined as any significant output or product that contributes directly and substantively within the first thirty plus days of war to the performance of a combat unit with a wartime mission. The point made here is that much centralized organizational output does not contribute, either directly or indirectly, to warfighting. It should also be noted that a definition of warfighting limited to organizations that make contributions within the first thirty plus days of war is reasonable in view of a competing strategies approach and the advantages that accrue to the side able to deploy conventional forces with mass, speed, and surprise in its favor.

Finally, it must be noted that current Army assets have the potential for a more cost-effective organization in terms of warfighting as well as the potential for higher performing units. Among the quality soldiers and NCOs already in the Army, from the tens of thousands of people currently working in jobs with little apparent contribution to Army warfighting and within current dollar limits, the Army has the potential to sharply increase its combat power through increased numbers of combat troops available for massing and also through improved unit performance. To accomplish this and allow the United States to better meet its strategic commitments the extraordinarily inefficient model under which the Army is presently organized needs to undergo major change. Most of all the basic assumption behind the organization of today's Army, that centralization is synonymous with efficiency, must be recognized as old dogma, proven false and incapable of maximizing the human potential of the U.S. Army. Unfortunately the Army's highly centralized personnel system is based on the explicit premise that "modern managerial practice centralizes personnel decision making because managers have discovered the value of human resource accounting."[3] Faceless legions of regulation writers, action coordinators, "iron majors," and bureaucrats have entrenched themselves in the

Pentagon and throughout the Army structure and are continuing to expand centralized control. Indicative of this is the recent decision to turn over the personnel structure to system technicians in place of the combat arms officers who have traditionally run it because they know best the warfighting purpose the MPT system is supposed to serve. For the first time ever, the Army's personnel system is being run, from the three-star Deputy Chief of Staff for Personnel down to division level G-1 staff officer, by Adjutant General Officers who are system technicians with loyalties, priorities, and vested interests in the centralized system but with little first-hand experience in the Army the system is supposed to serve. The recently created Total Army Personnel Agency (TAPA), which was renamed the Total Army Personnel Command in late 1988, was originally proposed to be a four-star command. It was to add even more information systems to the already more than 200 personnel management information systems currently necessary to support centralized decision makers. But such an increase goes against what we know about achieving efficacy in large organizations. Evidence is plentiful that highly centralized controls over policies (e.g., promotions, assignments, training, etc.) have been much less than fully effective in maximizing human productivity. Large organizations in a wide number of areas are now rapidly decentralizing in a variety of power-down modes in order to maximize the potential and productivity of the human element.

However, the Army continues to strengthen and pour additional money and people into its centralized headquarters. We have created a huge matrix organization where no one is in charge or responsible for the final product, which is war-ready units capable of meeting the highest standards. We have created many vertical and horizontal management structures that cut across the Army organization in support of various functions or subfunctions. For example, we have the Personnel Command and its various support agencies in charge of personnel, TRADOC with 100,000 personnel assigned and billions of dollars in charge of training the individual soldier, and various information commands in charge of providing necessary information. The whole management process is kept in motion with the Personnel Command shifting people endlessly and TRADOC attempting to train thousands of individuals to fill hundreds of moving specialties, leaving the unit commander with many valid excuses for poor performance. Who can hold a commander responsible when he can point to over 100 percent turbulence, 35 percent attrition, low-quality leadership, dated data, missing trained soldiers, and so on. This is the nature of matrix management in large centralized organizations. No one is really in charge and thus accountable for poor performance.

Meanwhile organizations like IBM, General Motors, the Tactical Air Command, and even the Communist Party and government of the Soviet Union have discovered the inefficiencies of large centralized organizations. It remains for the Army to discover that it has not been well served by the management theories of the 1960s and 1970s that taught the accounting efficiencies of consolidation and centralization. Prodded by the Japanese, American business has recognized the importance of the human element and how it is best motivated, led, and managed. A current Army slogan says that the soldier is the most important component of the system. If indeed soldiers are the most important part of the Army, little time should be lost in organizing to maximize the human potential offered by soldiers.

The changes necessary to improve combat performance and to increase the numbers of combat troops are straightforward, but bold adjustments in organization and policies are required. This book is not the place for a comprehensive recommendation but any solution should consider the following related points:

- The manpower spaces saved originally through centralized consolidation of the McNamara era have long since been exceeded by the enormous and continuous growth of centralized bureaucracy. The reduction or elimination of organizations that have limited contribution to warfighting can be the source of tens of thousands of spaces and hundreds of millions of dollars necessary to improve the Army's strategic capability to mass combat troops.
- Improved unit cohesion and unit performance would accompany sharply reduced turbulence, reassignment of quality NCOs from administrative to combat leadership positions, reduced attrition, and unit-based training. This would allow long-term cumulative training of high-performing units beyond the average one hundred days or less annually that 84 percent of officers and 80 percent of NCOs in Table of Equipment units now spend training in the field.

To quote from a recent article in *Parameters,* "Our Army is worn-out ... what's worn-out is our thinking — the fundamental ideas that give the Army its character and inform its basic policies."[4] Indeed, when the central personnel bureaucracy, for example, takes pride in and markets personnel turbulence as "big business" with "nearly half a million moves per year on nearly a billion dollar budget" without recognizing at the same time that this "business" is one of the biggest obstacles to improved unit performance, the Army is indeed in need of fresh thinking and new ideas.

New approaches that increase Army capability to mass combat power worldwide through increased numbers of combat troops in higher-performing units are possible within current strength levels and for less money. Such an approach requires that commanders be given responsibility for many of the MPT policies now centrally executed within the Army. This new Army would be characterized by few peacetime permanent transfers between units and organizations. Most soldiers, sergeants, and junior officers would spend almost all of their careers assigned to one home station in the United States. Maximum opportunity for unit training with consistent long-term high-quality unit leadership would produce first-class units. Commanders, units, and families would develop long-term community support systems primarily based in the private sectors, making possible spouses' careers (80 percent of American spouses expected to work in the 1990s) and home ownership.[5] Overseas deployment required by our worldwide strategic requirements would be greatly enhanced by this new approach to Army manpower, personnel, and training organization. Most overseas commitments would be met by small-unit deployments from the United States either through temporary duty or short overseas tours of up to one year. As proven by some Reforger exercises in Europe, units deployed in this manner can be more proficient and combat-ready than units already deployed to Europe on a long-term basis. With such short tours of duty, separations from home stations would not occur more than every three to five years for career soldiers and only once, if at all, for most soldiers. The long-term savings through discontinuing overseas family and permanent infrastructure support systems would be tremendous. Overseas infrastructure support systems could be devoted primarily to warfighting needs. Most importantly, data exist that show improved unit performance and warfighting capability would accompany such a system. Long-term cumulative training effects would allow units to raise levels of performance beyond the average to mediocre levels to which they have long been restricted. Improved overall unit readiness would be accompanied by an improved worldwide deployment posture to accompany the current European-oriented posture. Such a system would work with either a volunteer or draft Army and the regional, home station character of the new system could provide for elimination of the current training and organizational bottleneck restricting the Army's capability to mobilize rapidly and train a greatly expanded Army. Additional favorable indicators promise to be plentiful with such a system. Attrition, retention, balance of payments, cohesion, permanent change of station costs, reduced management systems costs, and other data all prompt change. The Army needs to think forward to manning the force in the 1990s and the twenty-first century unfettered by the business-as-usual and evolutionary approach to change, which dictates that tomorrow will be much the same as today.

NOTES

1. Peter W. Kuzumplik, summary of *Comparative Wartime Replacement Systems* (Washington, D.C.: Defense Intelligence Agency, 1986).

2. For an in-depth discussion of the goals and assumptions behind the rapid growth in the creation of the Army centralized management system for MPT, see Thomas E. Kelly, "Towards Excellence, The Army Develops a New Personnel System," manuscript submitted to Sloan School of Management, April 1983.

3. Ibid., 76–77.

4. A. J. Bacevich, "Old Myths, New Myths: Reviewing American Military Thought," *Parameters,* U.S. Army War College, March, 1988, 15.

5. For an example of much of what is proposed here, see briefing by Kent Eaton and Paul Gade on Home Station Concept of Personnel Management, Army Research Institute, Manpower Laboratory, August 1988.

BIBLIOGRAPHY

BOOKS

Binkin, Martin. *Military Technology and Defense Manpower*. Washington, D.C.: The Brookings Institution, 1986.

Bowman, WIlliam, Roger Little, and Thomas Sicilia. *The All-Volunteer Force After a Decade*. New York: Pergamon-Brassey's, 1986.

Clausewitz, Carl Von. *On War*. Translated by Michael Howard and Peter Parent. Princeton, N.J.: Princeton University Press, 1976.

Cohen, Eliot A. *Citizens and Soldiers*. Ithaca, N.Y.: Cornell University Press, 1985.

DePuy, William E. "Technology and Manpower: Army Perspective" in William Bowman, Roger Little, and Thomas Sicilia, eds., *The All-Volunteer Force After a Decade*. Washington, D.C.: Pergamon-Brassey's, 1983.

Dunn, Keith A., and William O. Staudenmaier. *Alternative Military Strategies for the Future*. Boulder, Colo.: Westview Press, 1985.

Foster, Gregory, Alan Sabrosky, and William Taylor. *The Strategic Dimension of Military Manpower*. Cambridge, Mass.: Harper and Row, 1987.

Gal, Reuven. *The Israeli Soldier*. Westport, Conn.: Greenwood Press, 1987.

Gilroy, Curtis L. *Army Manpower Economics*. Boulder, Colo.: Westview Press, 1986.

Henderson, William Darryl. *Cohesion: The Human Element in Combat*. Washington, D.C.: National Defense University Press, 1985.

___. *Why the Viet Cong Fought*. Westport, Conn.: Greenwood Press, 1985.

Holmes, Richard. *Firing Line*. Suffolk, Great Britain: Richard Clay, 1986.

Kelly, Thomas E. "Towards Excellence, The Army Develops a New Personnel System." Manuscript submitted to Sloan School of Management, April 1983.

Killebrew, Robert B. *Conventional Defense and Total Deferrence*. Wilmington, Del.: Scholarly Resources, Inc., 1986

Knorr, Klaus, and Patrick Morgan, eds. *Strategic Military Surprise*. New Brunswick, N.J.: 1982.

Kuzumplich, Peter W. *Comparative Wartime Replacement Systems*. Washington, D.C.: Defense Intelligence Agency, 1986.

Levy, Marion J. *The Structure of Society*. Princeton, N.J.: Princeton University Press, 1952.

Luttwak, Edward. *The Pentagon and the Art of War*. New York: Simon and Schuster, 1985.

Margiotta, Franklin D. et al. *Changing Military Manpower Realities*. Boulder, Colo.: Westview Press, 1983.

Marshall, S. L. A. *Men Against Fire*. New York: William Morrow, 1947.

Merton, Robert K. *Social Theory and Social Structure: Toward the Codification of Theory and Research*. Rev. Ed. Glencoe, Ill.: Free Press, 1957.

Moskos, Charles C., and Frank R. Wood, eds. *The Military — More Than Just a Job*. New York: Pergamon-Brassey's, 1988.

Record, Jeffery. *Revisiting U.S. Military Strategy*. McLean, Va.: Pergamon-Brassey's, 1984.

Turbulence Definition and Measurement. Vols. 1–3. McLean, Va.: General Research Corporation, 1982.

Wilson, Bennie J., III. *The Guard and Reserve in the Total Force*. Washington, D.C.: National Defense University Press, 1985.

GOVERNMENT DOCUMENTS

Boice, Lawrence R., and T. O. Jacobs. "Toward True Measures of Personnel Turbulence." Draft paper. Washington, D.C.: ARI, May 1988.

Brown, Frederic J. Preface to unpublished paper on "Combat Readiness for the Armor Force." Fort Knox, Ky.: U.S. Armor Center, July 1985.

"External Turbulence Report." Fort Benjamin Harrison, Ind.: U.S. Army Soldier Support Center, March 9, 1984.

Field Manual 100-5, Operations. Washington, D.C.: U.S. Army, 1982 and 1986 editions.

Hamburger, Kenneth E. "Leadership in Combat: An Historical Appraisal." West Point, N.Y.: U.S. Military Academy, Department of History, 1981.

"Leader Development Study." Fort Leavenworth, Kans.: U.S. Army Combined Arms Center, 1987.

McNair, L. J. Memorandum for General Marshall, Subject: Railey Investigation, General Headquarters, U.S. Army, October 14, 1941.

Malone, Dandridge M. "With the Mountain Men." ARI Report No. DAAL03-86-D-0001. Alexandria, Va.: ARI, 1988.

Marlowe, D. H. et al. "Unit Manning System Evaluation," Technical Reports Nos. 1 through 5. Washington, D.C.: Walter Reed Army Institute of Research, 1987.

Meyer, General E. C. *White Paper.* Washington, D.C.: Department of the Army, 1980.

Quinzi, Anthony J. "Personnel Turbulence in a Mechanized Infantry Battalion." APO New York 09114-5413: TRAC-WSMR Field Office, October 23, 1986.

Report of the Commission on Integrated Long-Term Strategy, "Discriminate Deterrence." Washington, D.C.: Government Printing Office, January 1988.

Report of the Secretary of Defense to Congress on the Fiscal Year 1988–1989 Budget and Fiscal Year 1989–1992 Defense Programs, January 12, 1987.

Sergeants Business. "NCO Professional Development: A Report to the NCO Corps." Washington, D.C.: Department of the Army, February 1986.

Shelyag, V. V., A. D. Glotochkin, and K. K. Platonov. "Military Psychology: A Soviet View." Moscow. Translated and published by the U.S. Air Force, Washington, D.C., 1972.

Siebold, Guy L. "Army Values: Results of Theme Year Research." Alexandria, Va.: ARI, January 1987.

Smith, Alfred L., Jr. "A Multivariate Analysis of Determinants Reenlistment: A Decision-Making Model for Enlisted Personnel." Working paper. Alexandria, Va.: ARI, March 1988.

Spurlock, Delbert L., Jr., Assistant Secretary of the Army (Manpower and Reserve Affairs), memo for Chief of Staff, U.S. Army. Subject: Army Image, July 14, 1988.

The Army Non Commissioned Officer Guide. Department of the Army, PM 22-600-20. Washington, D.C.: Government Printing Office, 1980.

Toomipuu, Juri. "Cost and Benefits of Quality Soldiers," USARECRN 86-1. Ft. Sheridan, Ill.: Army Recruiting Command, September 1986.

Word, Larry E. "Observations from Three Years at the National Training Center." Presidio of Monterey, Calif.: Army Research Institute Field Unit, January 1987.

PERIODICALS AND ARTICLES

Abramson, Rudy. "Eliminating Ballistic Missiles Dangerous." *Los Angeles Times*, December 6, 1986.

Abshire, David. Center for Strategic and International Studies report on the military balance, 1987, cited in *Newark Star-Ledger*, December 8, 1987, 44.

Ahearne, John F. "The Dark Side of War." *Washington Post*, August 23, 1987, B6.

Babiak, Paul. "On the Record." *Army Times*, May 30, 1988, 22.

Bacevich, A. J. "Old Myths, New Myths: Reviewing American Military Thought." *Parameters*, U.S. Army War College, March 1988.

Bahnsen, John C., and James W. Bradin. "The Army's Command Sergeant Major Problem." *Parameters*, June 1988.

Downs, Fred. "Death and the Dark Side of Command." *Washington Post*, Outlook section, August 16, 1988.

Famiglietti, Len. "NATO Leaves Technology in Laboratory." *Jane's Defense Weekly*, November 28, 1987, 1245.

Galvin, General John R., Supreme Commander Allied Forces, Europe, cited by Henry Vanloon, *Armed Forces Journal*, March 1988.

Goldsmith, John A. "Manpower: A Weak Link?" *Military Logistics Forum*, April 1987, 32.

Golioto, Joseph. "Organizational Culture and Readiness in the Reserve Components." Research Directorate, National Defense University, Ft. McNair, Washington, D.C., 1986.

"Growth of NCO Ranks Outstrips Total Enlisted in Recent Years." *Army Times,* February 8, 1988, 4, 24.

Guidry, Vernon A., Jr. "Memo by General Says Army's Wartime Reserve Plan Won't Work." *Baltimore Sun,* September 16, 1986, 1.

Henderson, Wm. Darryl. "Can-Do NCOs — With Clout — Can Help Cohesion Problems." *Army,* March 1982.

"Here's How E-7 Stripes Fell by MOS." *Army Times,* February 9, 1987, 12.

Herrly, John. "Midweight Force Needed Now More than Ever." *Army Times,* May 15, 1989, 23.

Kreisher, Otto. "U.S. Pullback from 3 1/2 War Strategy Seen." *San Diego Union,* January 13, 1987, 1.

Leuer, Kenneth C. "More Boots on Ground." *Army Times,* March 14, 1988, 10.

Matthews, William. "U.S. Seen Poorly Equipped for Low-Intensity Wars." *Army Times,* December 8, 1986, 12.

Meyer, Deborah G. "More Authority Responsibility Placed on NCOs' Shoulder at Fort Hood." *Armed Forces Journal,* May 1985, 74.

Pentagram, December 4, 1986, 3.

Philips, Robert et al. Unpublished paper. "Combat Readiness for the Armor Force." Fort Knox, Ky.: U.S. Armor Center, 1985, 2–13.

Record, Jeffery. *Armed Forces Journal,* October 1987.

Recruiter Journal. Chicago: USAREC, March 11, 1988, 1.

Rowland, David. "Assessments of Combat Degradation." *RUSI,* June 1986.

Schemmer, Benjamin F. "Army Planning Revealed at its Worst." *Armed Forces Journal,* April 1987, 14

Schrage, Michael. "The Sword of Science." *Washington Post Magazine,* October 9, 1983, 22–23.

Shields, Joyce. "The Army's Quality Need." In Robert Philips et al., eds. Unpublished paper. "Combat Readiness for the Armor Force." Fort Knox, Ky.: U.S. Armor Center, 1985, 2–9.

Smith, K. R. "Dimensions of Morale." Armidale NSW, Australia: Armidale College, 1987.

"Paper Chase." *Soldiers,* July 1985.

Spurlock, Delbert L. "On the Record." *Army Times,* October 17, 1988, 22.

Tice, Jim. "Reenlistments Ease the Pain of Bearish Recruiting Market." *Army Times,* April 17, 1989, 6.

Wilson, George C. "Army Faces Deep Personnel Cuts to Pay for Arms." *Washington Post,* February 11, 1988, 4.

___. "In Mock Combat, 'Soviets' Win Again and Again." *Washington Post,* February 22, 1982, A8.

___. "U.S. Reserves Called Insufficient for War in Europe." *Wasington Post,* April 14, 1988, 9.

Wood, David. "Kremlin Stealthily Amasses Strike Force in Europe." *Newark Star-Ledger,* December 8, 1987, 44.

INDEX

ABOUT THE AUTHOR

WM. DARRYL HENDERSON, Colonel (ret.) U.S. Army, graduated with a B.A. from Stanford University in 1961, which included a year at the University of Vienna, Austria, studying history. He received a Ph.D. in comparative political systems and international relations from the University of Pittsburgh in 1974. Additionally, Dr. Henderson served as an assistant professor and instructor in international relations, comparative systems, and military psychology at West Point. He is a graduate of the Army's Command and General Staff College and the National War College, where he was also a senior research fellow.

Among his publications are: *Cohesion: The Human Element in Combat* (NDU Press, 1985); *Why the Viet Cong Fought: A Study of Motivation and Control in a Modern Army in Combat* (Greenwood Press, 1973); coauthor and regional editor, *Handbook of World Conflicts* (University of Pittsburgh Press, 1970).

Dr. Henderson was an infantryman and served in a variety of assignments including three years as an infantry company commander (including one in Vietnam), numerous infantry battalion and brigade staff assignments, Battalion Command, assistant professor, Social Sciences Department, and instructor for leadership and military psychology at West Point; deputy commander, Joint Security Area, Panmunjom, Korea; staff assistant in the Office of Deputy Secretary of Defense; executive assistant to the assistant secretary of Defense Legislative Affairs; Office of the Chief of Staff; with the Deputy Chief of Staff for Operations; and as a senior advisor to a major Army Reserve Command. Dr. Henderson recently served as a senior arms control planner on the International Military Staff, Headquarters NATO, followed by his most recent assignment as commander of the U.S. Army Research Institute in Washington, D.C. He retired from the U.S. Army on September 1, 1988. He is a parachutist and expert infantryman. His decorations include: the Legion of Merit, Bronze Star Medal, Purple Heart, and the Combat Infantryman's Badge.